Essential
Crete

by

ADAM HOPKINS

Adam Hopkins is a travel writer and regular
contributor to the *Sunday Times* and
The Guardian. He is the author of books
on Holland and Crete.

Produced by AA Publishing

Written by Adam Hopkins
Verified by
Christopher Somerville
Peace and Quiet section
by Paul Sterry

Revised third edition 1996
First published 1990

Edited, designed and produced by
AA Publishing.
© The Automobile Association 1990,
1994, 1994 (reprinted), 1996
Maps © The Automobile Association
1990, 1994, 1994 (reprinted), 1996

Distributed in the United Kingdom by
AA Publishing, Norfolk House,
Priestley Road, Basingstoke,
Hampshire, RG24 9NY.

A CIP catalogue record for this book
is available from the British Library.

ISBN 0 7495 1317 9

Published by AA Publishing, a
trading name of Automobile
Association Developments Limited,
whose registered office is Norfolk
House, Priestley Road, Basingstoke,
Hampshire,
RG24 9NY.
Registered number 1878835.

Colour Origination by:
L.C. Repro & Sons Ltd, Aldermaston,
England

Printed by: Printers S.R.L., Trento,
Italy

Front cover picture: *Agia Galini*

Contents

This book employs a simple rating system to help choose which places to visit:

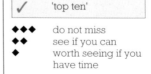

✓	'top ten'

◆◆◆	do not miss
◆◆	see if you can
◆	worth seeing if you have time

Greek place names can be transcribed in various ways and some appear in the text in two different forms. Where this occurs, the version in brackets is the form used on the maps.

INTRODUCTION

Crete is an island which is truly special, one of the strong places of the earth. Few can visit it, even for simple sun and sea, and return to their homes indifferent. Its people are dignified and generous; its mountains are rugged and visible everywhere; its fertile spots, though fewer, have a luxurious abundance. The island is lapped by many miles of beach, particularly along the north, with bay and cliff as dramatic interludes. It has a past which goes back well before the conscious memory of man.

The Minoans flourished here centuries before classical Greece. Theirs was the earliest of the great civilisations on European soil; and one of the pleasures of a visit to Crete is to make the acquaintance of their art and artefacts and the remains of their fine buildings. This was the civilisation which made a cult of the wild bull and gave rise to the extraordinary legends of Minos, the Minotaur and the Labyrinth of Knossos. Crete had great importance in classical mythology. The ancient Greeks left ruins behind them here as well as the Minoans. So did the Romans and the Byzantines, the Venetians who ruled the island for four centuries, and the Turks who held power for a further two. The modern Cretans, successors to this great avalanche of history, only became part of the modern Greek nation in 1913.

Ancient Crete was fertile and wealthy. Modern Crete is mostly harsh and rocky; World War II brought outright tragedy to a poor land. The defeat of the Allies here was followed by bitter repression under the Germans as the Cretans strove to wage a war of resistance. Better times have come just lately, however, with the arrival of international tourism. Through all this the Cretans have maintained a tradition of hospitality and welcome which appears to go back in an unbroken line, for three millennia at least, to the Bronze Age of the eastern Mediterranean. Crete has still in many ways and places the largeness of spirit evident in the epic tales of Homer – not that anyone should form too favourable an advance picture. Some of the best aspects of Crete are slow to reveal themselves. The splendour of the mountains may be felt at once, but the island is hot in summer and certainly seems dusty if you arrive in Irakleío, the capital. And Irakleio is astonishingly ugly. Many of Crete's hotels – the great majority of them along the beaches and bays of the north coast – are fine and comfortable, but some of the more recent building in tourist areas is flimsy, brash and uncoordinated. Along the south coast, and now creeping into parts of the north, there are multitudinous greenhouses covered in plastic sheeting which decays in winter. Moreover, the island is so rugged and parts of it still so inaccessible, despite a rapid improvement in the roads, that even with the best will in the world it would take many weeks to see every corner. Yet it is often in the most out-of-the-way places that Crete remains at its finest.

These are the complicating factors. In practice, most people take their first steps towards the deeper Crete within a very few days or hours, either through the discovery of landscape and villages or through their meetings with local people. Often, departing visitors, brown as berries from the beach, rate the friendliness of the Cretans beyond all the other pleasures of the island. For better or worse, those who come to know Crete well are never quite free of it again.

BACKGROUND

The Landscape

It is hard to make sense of Crete without some understanding of its unusual and dramatic physical construction. The island is long and thin – some 150 miles (250km) from east to west and 10 miles (15km) or so to 40 miles (60km) wide. Often known as the *Megali Nisi* or Great Island, it is easily the largest of the Greek islands. There are three main towns strung out along the northern coast – Chaniá in the extreme west, Réthymno in centre west and Irakleío, considerably the largest, almost at dead centre. The true tourist capital, though, is Ágios Nikólaos, halfway along towards the eastern end and looking out over a wide gulf. Agreeable little Siteía, to the east, was formerly one of the main towns, but it is hard to rate in the top league today. The major towns of the north coast and the coastal plain which links them, effectively from west of Chaniá to Ágios Nikólaos in the east, together have the bulk of the population and welcome the majority of tourists. Visually, though, it is the mountains which dominate. Being made of limestone, they are rugged and austere, mountainous far beyond their real size in the impression they create. As with the major towns, the mountain ranges come in a set of four. The finest and by far the wildest are the White Mountains or Lefká Óri in the west, lying more or less south of Chaniá. This is a terrain of gorges, crags and screes, treacherous to the inexperienced walker, inspiring to those who get to know its ways. Like most of the ranges, it hides high flat plains close to its heart.

Next along towards the centre of the island, lying well back from the coast between Réthymno and Irakleío, there rises the bulk of Psiloreitis (once better known as Ida), more a single mountain than a range, though pierced by extremely attractive high valleys. The highest peak of Psiloreitis is by a whisker the highest point on Crete – 8,058 feet (2,456m) compared to the 8,045 feet (2,452m) of Pachnes, top spot in the White Mountains. The lofty clump of mountain surging up south and west of Ágios Nikólaos is the Dikte massif.

Tourism and tradition: an old way of life meets new demands

Both Psiloreitis and Dikte possess caves which are immensely important in classical Greek myth; and Dikte also possesses in the Lasíthiou Plateau, right in its centre, the most extensive and remarkable of Crete's high plains. The southern part of the massif is particularly beautiful.

The final range, lower but still impressive, is round Siteía in the east. The mountains here hide interesting villages and lesser known prehistoric and historic sites. In many of the villages ancient ways of life persist.

From anywhere in Crete, and especially from the beaches, you are likely to see at least one of these ranges. Mountains, one feels, are what matter most in Crete. The richest part of the island agriculturally, however, lies south of the main mountain groups, in the central area of Crete. This is the Plain of Mesará, with huge and ancient olive trees and now many younger ones as well. The visitor will cross the Mesará to reach some of Crete's finest archaeological sites and, towards the west, a good view of innumerable plastic greenhouses. These produce several crops a year, running well ahead of the seasons. Among the crops are tomatoes, cucumbers, melons, and even kiwi fruit; bananas also grow profusely in Cretan greenhouses. In addition to the Mesará, there are other smaller areas which are also extremely fertile, their sense of ease and abundance contrasting most forcefully with the rigour of the rest of the island. Apart from the greenhouse crops, Crete's traditional staples are grapes and the ubiquitous lowland olive. Carob trees, smaller than olives and yielding dark-coloured, bean-like pods, are also very common, especially in the east. The beans are used mainly for animal fodder.

Crete's most extensive beaches lie along the northern coast where tourist development is concentrated. There are many miles of sand, some sand and shingle, some areas of rock well used by swimmers. Both the extreme east and west coasts have a few outstanding beaches though some of these are less accessible. There are pockets of exceedingly fine beach along the south of the island.

The Rise of the Minoans

Something extraordinary began to happen in Crete almost 5,000 years ago, in about 3000 BC. Perhaps it was to do with the seclusion of the island, the distances of sea that had to be traversed by new arrivals; perhaps it was in part the natural wealth of the land – Crete in ancient times was thickly forested and well-watered; perhaps it was to do with the nature of the island's first inhabitants or of the new immigrants now joining them from the east. Whatever the reason, from nearly imperceptible beginnings, a highly individual civilisation took shape.

Neolithic people had first reached Crete some 3,000 years before, in about 6000 BC. Their main settlement was at Knossos, near modern Irakleio. Otherwise they lived mostly in caves and refuges. But round about 2600 BC, many settlements moved down to the sea, suggesting a new confidence and sense of security. This was indispensable for future developments. Perhaps the most important characteristic of the whole Minoan civilisation is that its development appears to have gone hand in hand with peace and prosperity. Its artists, so far as is known, never showed scenes of war; its towns and, later, its palaces, were undefended. The early Minoans (as we know them now), flourishing particularly in the east and then a little later in the Mesará, were brilliant potters. They carved beautiful stone jars, some with lively animal motifs, and worked in ivory and rock crystal. From an early period they were making quite remarkable, and amazingly beautiful, miniature designs on sealstones. Pottery is the great standby in understanding and discussing prehistoric societies. It is the most durable of materials, and the least likely to be removed from any site, having little value compared to jewellery or weapons and none at all when it is broken. It was used by archaeologists in Crete as elsewhere for the dating of other artefacts and establishing the sequence of developments. This makes it seem natural to open discussion of Minoan periods by talking of pottery styles. But an even better reason is that the pottery from most Minoan periods was exceptionally lovely.

Only 600 years from its beginning, Minoan society was constructing a series of vast palaces. Some of the great triumphs of the Minoan potters were achieved in the time of the first palaces, from 1900 to 1700 BC; there are many examples in the Archaeological Museum in Irakleío.

Work in other art forms also proliferated. Jewellery of the 'Old Palace' period is wonderfully intricate and clear. Sealstone carving continued to develop. Metalwork generally, and the production of weapons in particular, reached an exceedingly high standard. In shrines on mountain peaks and deep in caves, worshippers of the Minoan deities left behind vigorous and delightful miniature sculptures.

The Minoan 'New Palaces'

While all this great profusion was at its height, at about 1700 BC, all the palaces were destroyed to their foundations, apparently all at once and most probably by earthquake. But almost at once the Minoans were able to pick themselves up and to construct a fresh set of palaces, even larger and more elaborate than their predecessors, on the same sites. These are the 'New Palaces', mighty buildings whose ruins can still be seen today at Knossos and Phaistos and in slightly more modest form at Málía and Káto Zákros. With their construction, architecture now steps to the fore as the leading art form. Some of the palaces were on several storeys, with theatrical-looking steps and performance areas outside, great staircases mounting within and characteristic inverted pillars, thicker at the top than at the bottom. Walls were lined with the finest materials and decorated with the frescos which are a familiar trademark of the Minoans. Even in ruins, the great palaces are extraordinary and evocative places, but they are also baffling and can be disconcerting. Maybe this is simply because they *are* ruins and difficult to interpret, but it is conceivable that they are not what they seem. The accepted view is that the palaces were the homes of the Minoan ruling class, probably one, or possibly several, royal families. The palaces formed the pivot of state and religious life, and were the venue for the famous bull-leaping

The exuberance of a ceremony held thousands of years ago is captured in a bull-leaping fresco in Irakleío's Archaeological Museum

ceremonies; in short, they were full of life and richness. But there is another view, and it is that these were actually palaces of the dead, inhabited only by those performing the rites that would satisfy the gods, or the spirits of the dead. Classical archaeologists reject the theory, but it has precedents in Egyptian tombs, for example, and Neolithic burial places elsewhere in Europe. No one knows, and there are many who would rather not know.

About the spiritual and social workings of Minoan civilisation, precious little is known – even from seemingly straightforward objects. The Minoan bull is ever-present and must have represented some aspect of divinity – perhaps the earth and earthquakes; the leading divinity seems to have been a goddess, mistress of the animals, close to the heart of nature.

Women in Minoan palace society appear to have had a high position. So many works of art are to do with sports or pleasure that it has often been argued that this must also have been an unusually playful society, at peace with itself as well as with its neighbours. It is clear that Crete was an important trading nation, and probably an important maritime power. Certainly, this is what later Greek historians like Thucydides believed.

As for ordinary people, it is likely that they lived in a very simple way in crowded towns. The population of Minoan Crete may have been very large. We do not know how society was governed or what the relationship was between palaces and towns. There is a distinct impression of two levels of society with a wide division between them. We can say with certainty that those involved in the palace society lived in the presence of some of the most beautiful art objects ever made. All this came to an end, through most of Crete, in about 1450 BC, when the 'New' Palaces were two and a half centuries old. Káto Zákros, Mália and Phaistos were destroyed. Knossos was partly destroyed, was then repaired and staggered on for perhaps another 70 years. What happened has been a matter of the keenest conjecture. The original theory was that the palaces had been destroyed by attackers, perhaps the Achaians (or Acheans) also known as

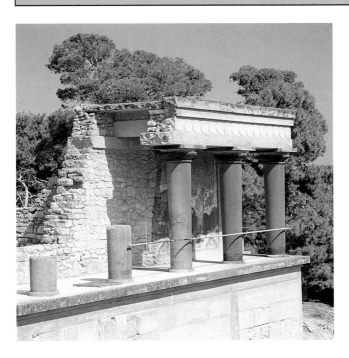

At Knossos, parts of the New Palace (now restored) have survived for over 3,000 years; its predecessor was razed to the ground

Myceneans, mainland Greeks from the north. These are the people of whom buried memories persist in the epics of Homer, which were composed centuries later and written down centuries later again. But it was also known that the island of Santorini north of Crete, itself a Minoan colony, had been destroyed by a mighty volcanic eruption at about that time. So the second theory of the destruction of the palaces pinned the blame on Santorini. The current belief among archaeologists is that the Santorini eruption occurred 50 years earlier than the catastrophe and that the fall of Minoan Crete was indeed the responsibility of attackers. This theory seems to be supported by evidence drawn from language and writing. A script in linear form (known as Linear A) was developed quite early on during the Minoan period and was used to write in a language which has not yet been read. A new language came in at about the end of the New Palace period (written in hieroglyphics called Linear B) with many inscriptions surviving on tablets. After much scholarly argument, it has now been accepted that the language written in Linear B was an early form of Greek. This makes it virtually certain that a Greek-speaking people was dominant in Knossos during its final years. Certainly we know from Greek myth of the central importance of Crete to the ancient Greeks both as a home of the gods and the home of Minos and the Minotaur.

Crete in Myth

For the ancient Greeks, whose civilisation reached its height 1,000 years after the collapse of the Minoan, there were essentially two sets of myths about Crete. One concerned Zeus, the leading figure in the Greek pantheon. The belief that associated him so strongly with Crete made the island a holy place for the Greeks. The other set of myths concerned Minos, and may have contained, however deeply buried, some fragments of a genuine tradition passed on by the Achaians.

Zeus was generally believed in the ancient world to have been born in a cave on Crete, the son of Rhea and the monstrous figure Kronos. There was also a Cretan belief that Zeus was dead and buried on Mt Youktas, a peak just behind Irakleio. From a certain angle Youktas has an uncanny look of a helmeted warrior. A number of other Greek gods and goddesses are associated with Crete and there are hosts of secondary figures. One of the most interesting is the bronze giant Talos who ran continually round the coast destroying those who attempted to land there. In some versions, he was finally betrayed and killed by Medea, sorceress and wife of Jason, as she and Jason and the other Argonauts returned to Greece at the end of their quest for the Golden Fleece. Stories of Minos tell of two brothers – Minos and Rhadmanthys, both kings and lawgivers. Minos ruled in Knossos, Rhadmanthys perhaps in Phaistos. Every nine years Minos went to a sacred cave and met Zeus face to face. His wife, Pasiphae, fell in love with a bull, and their offspring was a beast called the Minotaur, so terrible that he had to be confined in a labyrinth at Knossos, purpose-built by the great engineer Daidalos (Daedalus). Young men and women were brought each year from Athens to be devoured by the Minotaur, until Theseus, son of King Aegeus, joined the prospective victims and killed the beast. The story goes that upon his arrival at Knossos, Minos's daughter Ariadne fell in love with the Athenian prince. She gave him a ball of thread which he unwound behind him as he made his way through the labyrinth to the Minotaur's lair. By following the thread, Theseus escaped and fled with Ariadne, though he later abandoned her on the Island of Naxos. Then he and his companions sailed for Athens. The plan was that they should hoist a white sail in place of black as a signal of success. (Black would mean that Theseus was dead.) But they forgot to make the change and King Aegeus, mistakenly believing his son dead, threw himself into the sea when he saw the black sail. Since then the sea has been called the Aegean in his honour.

Jason and the Argonauts are guided through the night by Tiphys. Jason's wife Medea was said to have killed Crete's bronze giant Talos

Daidalos the engineer had helped Ariadne in the plot against the Minotaur and he too had to flee from Crete. He constructed two sets of wings, with feathers held in place by wax. One was for himself, one for his son Ikaros (Icarus). Daidalos flew successfully, but Ikaros flew too close to the sun – with fatal consequences. The wax melted and he plunged into the sea. Minos, when he died, went down to the underworld and took up duties there as lawgiver to the dead.

There are many references to Crete in the *Odyssey* and the *Iliad*, attributed to the blind poet Homer and dating from about 900 BC. He tells of a powerful king named Idomeneos, grandson of Minos, who took a Cretan fleet to the Trojan wars. Homer's stories and place names, so it appears today, are derived from oral tradition based on the Myceneans or Achaians who inhabited mainland Greece from the time of the late Minoans and flourished for several centuries after that. These, of course, were the very people who had probably conquered Minoan Crete. He refers to Crete as 'fair and fertile' and mentions 90 cities, some of them by name. He also refers to an indigenous Cretan people who may have been the last of the Minoans, living on under Mycenean rule.

Crete in History

The Myceneans/Achaians, who were the dominant force at the end of the Minoan period, were replaced by a new set of Greek-speaking arrivals, the Dorians from the north. They built stout citadels, many of which survive as impressive ruins. They also made handsome, simple sculpture of a kind called Daidalic – immensely important in helping to start up the sculptural tradition of classical Greece – and organised themselves into small city-states in a way that prefigured the classical Greek world. They were extremely conservative by temperament and may have passed on their own form of social organisation to Sparta in the Peloponnese.

Next came the Romans, who took over the island in 67 BC after three years of bitter campaigning. The Roman period in Crete, which lasted four centuries, was prosperous and settled. Then, from the late 4th century,

The Byzantine influence in Crete outlasted Byzantine rule, and was strikingly expressed in chapel frescos such as this one in Kritsá

when Constantine moved the capital of the empire to Constantinople (modern Istanbul), Crete, by now Christian, came under eastern influence. It remained in the Byzantine world for most of 900 years – with one extremely significant interruption.

In AD 824 Crete was captured and occupied by Arab raiders, who destroyed the Roman basilicas and a good deal else besides. In 961 the Byzantines, led by the future emperor Nikephoras Phokas, retook the island amid scenes of the greatest violence. Nikephoras Phokas is remembered today in street names in many Cretan towns. Under the Byzantine rule which ensued, art-forms manifested themselves most beautifully with the construction of rural chapels, decorated with frescos. The frescos showed God the ruler of all, known as the Pantocrator; Jesus, Mary and the saints; and a host of stories from the Christian canon, all in a ritualised arrangement and in the strange hierarchical perspective of the Byzantines. This strong tradition was maintained for centuries, long after Byzantine rule had ended. Only a few frescos have been restored but they remain an important and sometimes moving aspect of an exploration of Crete.

After the sack of Constantinople in 1204, dominance in Crete passed first to the Genoese and then to the Venetian empire. The Venetians took timber from the island, accelerating a process of deforestation which finally wiped out almost all the cypress forests for which the island had been famous. For the Cretans themselves, the long Venetian period (1210 to 1669) was a hard and bitter time. They were virtually slaves, ferociously repressed and often in rebellion. The Venetians built strong defences in the major towns and a number of fine castles all round the island, both to repel invaders and to quell the populace. Though often ruined, almost all of these survive and are one of the great features of the island.

Crete's history has been one of foreign rule and rebellion. In the 19th century there were many uprisings against the Turkish rulers

During long wars in the mid-17th century, the Turks captured most of the island and Irakleío itself – known then as El Khandak or Candia – was finally taken in 1669 after a 20-year siege. This ushered in the most desperate period of Cretan history. Turkish rule was arbitrary and capricious. There were many revolts, most notably that of Ioannis Daskaloyiannis in 1770. Many Cretans converted to Islam. During the 19th century as the Greek independence movement gained strength on the mainland, the Cretans indulged in their own rebellions, and the long revolutionary tradition of the island was strengthened at immeasurable cost in blood and destruction.

Although the modern Greek state originated in 1832, Crete remained firmly in Turkish hands till the end of the century. It came briefly under joint rule by Russia, France, Britain and Italy, and until recently it was possible to meet old people in Réthymno who remembered Russian occupation of their town. Finally, the murder in Irakleío of 14 British soldiers and the British consul brought Turkish rule to an end. But it was not until 1913, and after further bitter political struggles, that Crete officially became part of Greece.

Peace lasted until 1922, when following Greece's defeat in a war against Turkey, Greeks living on the west coast of Turkey were exchanged for Turks still resident in Greece. This transfer of populations has given Crete the homogeneous Greek character which distinguishes it so sharply from Cyprus. In World War II Crete was once more a place of bitter struggle. The Italians entered Albania and were held there by the Greeks. Then the Germans came into the contest, rolling up not just the Greek army but also the Allied expeditionary force that had been sent to the Greek mainland. Both forces, Greek and Allied, now retreated to Crete and joined the Allied garrison holding the island. Within a pitifully brief period the Germans had caught up with them again and the Battle of Crete began. It lasted barely a week. The island's defences were poorly organised. German dominance of the air was total, and British naval ships from Egypt could not get into the crucial northern ports without exposing themselves to air attack. On 20 May 1941, German gliders and paratroops swooped on all the airfields of the north coast – Irakleío, Réthymno and Máleme in the west. They were held in Irakleío and Réthymno but in Máleme they opened up a chink and little by little forced their way out through it to turn the Allied retreat into a rout. The battle had been a terrible one and now the Allies staged a fearful march across the mountains to be taken off from the southern coast by British ships. The Greeks, who had fought heroically, were simply abandoned and so, finally, were 5,000 Allied troops when the navy could no longer get in to the little port of Hora Sfakion where they were trapped. These men were either captured or sheltered by Cretans and many later managed to escape. That any of them had even got as far as Sfákia, was due to a Greek regiment on the far side of the mountains which held the German forces and provided an escape route. During the Battle of Crete many bands of freelance warriors sprang into existence and these, together with Allied operatives later put ashore on Crete, now formed the nucleus of increasingly determined and well-organised resistance.

Tales of Cretan heroism between 1941 and the war's end are legion, and in one stunning propaganda *coup* the German general on Crete was captured and spirited off the island by the well-organised resistance – an event celebrated in the famous film *Ill Met by Moonlight*.

After the war, Crete was extremely poor and life returned to normality only very slowly. Many of the young men were obliged to leave in search of work. By the 1960s, however, tourism began to make an impact. Changes have since been very swift and much of the development is unplanned and lacks cohesion. It is visibly the case, however, that many tourist enterprises are small enough and local enough for the benefits to have spread out surprisingly widely. In the light of Crete's bitter modern history, it is hard to resent the island's current good fortune. At the same time, one cannot fail to notice the contrast between the tourist strip on some parts of the northern coast and the achievements of the Minoans thousands of years before.

CENTRAL CRETE

Ágios Nikólaos, away to the east, is the most populous individual resort in Crete, and Chaniá in the west impresses many as the finest. But Irakleío and its large district, right in the centre, are cumulatively the most visited. Irakleío itself is by far the largest town on the island. Knossos, the main Minoan site, is near by; and the Archaeological Museum (Arkheologikó Mousío), with the best from all the ancient Minoan sites in Crete, is in town. Except for the Archaeological Museum in Athens, this is the largest and finest in Greece – and, of course, it has the finest Minoan collection anywhere. Phaistos, the most important

Agía Ekaterini church nestles beside the 19th-century cathedral

Minoan palace after Knossos, is in the southern part of central Crete, flanked by the lovely Minoan site at Agía Triáda and by later, extensive ruins at Gortyn. All of these places are in the rich Plain of Mesará, overlooked by the bulk of Mount Psiloreitis. Irakleío is not a resort. Most visitors to the centre stay in hotels along the beaches of the north coast, specially in Hersonisos and Mália. Rather fewer stay in the central south, though the fine beaches and man-made caves of Mátala have attracted fame of a sort, and Agía Galíni, a crowded little resort on the south coast, is not far distant in the prefecture of Réthymno.

IRAKLEÍO

Those who are accustomed to Middle Eastern towns will not be surprised by Irakleío, fifth city of

Greece, and undisputed centre of Cretan life. It is a place of concrete and flat roofs, a noisy, sprawling, dusty, active, 20th-century kind of city, not at all what one might expect as point of entry to an island of sea and beaches, snow-white chapels and the extraordinary wealth of antiquities which helps to make Crete a place apart. Yet there Irakleío stands, right in the middle, with the island's principal port at its heart and the island's main airport just out to the east. It is almost impossible to avoid the city while visiting Crete. Many are drawn by the Archaeological Museum, the world's main showplace for Minoan artefacts; or they pass through to visit the neighbouring Minoan site of Knossos.

Backpackers and other visitors off the ferries, however, may well spend a night or two here before moving on, and the city's rather mediocre lodging houses are crammed in summer. But, however they come and however long they stay, almost all visitors are mildly shocked at first by Irakleío. Although it is per capita the wealthiest city in Greece, it remains more than a little drab and dingy.

There is, however, a surprising amount to see. Crete's greatest concentration of professional people may be seen at work and play in and around Irakleío. Villagers come in from a wide area to sell their produce, buy provisions or deal with money matters. The city seems almost relaxed, certainly at its most genial, at the hour of the *volta*, the communal evening stroll. The central part of Irakleío is a walled town with massive Venetian ramparts generally invisible among houses or other obstructions. Visitors entering the city from any landward point must somehow pierce the ramparts to reach the middle. There are handsome and massive Venetian gates in the west (the Chaniá Pórta) and in the south (the 'new' or Kenoúria Pórta), through which passes Odhos Evans (Evans Street), a name famous in archaeology (see **Knossos**, below).

Those arriving from the east, from Ágios Nikólaos or the airport, will follow the main road through miles of dreary outskirts, then suddenly ascend a steep bend through the ramparts to find themselves in a semi-circular 'square', leafy but traffic-ridden, ringed on the far side with cafés and restaurants. This is the **Platía Eleftherias**, or Freedom Square, a gathering point from which the city radiates westwards. In one corner stands the Archaeological Museum with the main tourist office opposite.

From the **Platía Eleftherias**, the Odhos Dhikeosinis (Dikheosinis Street) leads to the square named for the Byzantine emperor Nikephoras Phokas. This is the true centre of town. If you now face towards the sea, directly behind you is the main market of Irakleío, in a crowded little street named Odhos 1866.

Directly in front, a bigger street leads to the old harbour, with long harbour mole and vast and somewhat blank Venetian fortress. To your left from Nikephoras Phokas, the main road winds away towards the Chaniá Pórta.

The **market of Irakleío** is a fine little scrimmage of a place, with vegetables and herbs and sponges, clasp knives, shoes and sausages, a seemingly casual collection of all kinds of bits and pieces, representing many aspects of island life. It is hot and somewhat exhausting in summer but cheerful and energetic at all times of year. Up past the market the **Platía Kornarou** (Kornarou Square) has a large statue of Erotokritos and Arethousa, hero and heroine of a massive 17th-century epic poem by one Vincenzos Kornaros – for whom the square is named. Kornaros was from Siteía in the east and his poem

The liveliest place in Irakleío: its bustling market, where you can buy virtually anything

The Erotokritos is a symbol of identity for Cretans and many other Greeks, the equivalent of a cross between Shakespeare and *Rule Britannia* for the British. There is also a fine fountain in the square. Returning to Nikephoras Phokas and turning left along Kalokerinou, the main road leading towards the Chaniá Pórta, then left again quite shortly, one reaches an open space bounded on the far side by the city's large 19th-century cathedral – not a thing of particular beauty. But this space also contains the Sinaiite church of St Katherine, **Agía Ekaterini**, with its fine collection of paintings (see page 28).

To the north from Nikephoras Phokas is the road towards the harbour. The open space almost immediately entered, replete with restaurants, fountain, pie shop and newsagent, is technically named the **Platía Venizelou** (Square of Venizelos) after the Cretan-born statesman who was Greek prime minister for many years and ushered Crete into the modern nation in 1913. Foreigners know it as 'Fountain Square'. The Kríni tou Morosini at its centre is Venetian, built in 1628 but incorporating a set of delightfully worn-out 14th-century lions. Almost immediately, to the right, is a reconstructed Venetian church, Ágios Márkos. This is followed very shortly by the reconstructed Venetian Loggia now used as the city hall. Tucked in behind, in a pretty little open space, is the church of Ágios Títos. The main road, Odhos Avgoustou 25 (August 25 Street) now leads on down towards the

port, passing Párko El Greco. The Cretan painter Domenico Theotokopoulos, 1541–1614, moved from Irakleío to Italy in his 20s and finally to Spain where he was known, of course, as El Greco, 'the Greek'. After a short walk, August 25 debouches on the old harbour, with the fortress opposite.

What to See in Irakleío

◆◆◆
ARCHAEOLOGICAL MUSEUM (ARKHEOLOGIKÓ MOUSÍO) ✓

Eleftherías Square
This is undoubtedly the star attraction of Irakleío, despite its ageing, shoddy building and surging summer crowds. In the days before mass seaside holidays, this museum, along with the palaces of Knossos and Phaistos, was considered the main reason for visiting Crete. It still remains central to the pleasure and understanding of many visitors.

It is best to go early or at lunchtime, in the hope of beating the worst of the crush. After some palace visiting, it is doubly rewarding to return to the museum for a slow perusal, matching a growing sense of Minoan art, architecture and stylistic change against the known flow of events.

The display is set out in rough chronological order from galleries I to XII, covering the ground from Neolithic and early Minoan, right through the height of the Minoan period and then out again into the post-palatial and Dorian era. A major gallery of Minoan sarcophagi is followed

A late Minoan pot decorated with papyrus flowers

by a centrally important exhibition of Minoan frescos, and, when it is open, by a fine collection of Minoan artefacts assembled by a private individual, one Dr Giamalakis. After this the museum again picks up the chronological story, the final rooms covering Greek and Roman antiquity.

It is astonishing to see just how rich and prolific the earliest Minoan periods were (mainly in gallery I). There were several distinctive pottery types. Vassiliki ware is the most interesting, usually jugs with overlong spouts and an odd 'flamed' effect where the clay has been mottled by

uneven application of fire, perhaps with a burning bunch of twigs. There are beautiful stone jars and intriguing stone boxes. Two of these, one a complete box and one merely a lid, show long leggy dogs sprawled across their surfaces, a high point of Minoan naturalism. This gallery also contains a fascinating range of jewellery and sealstones, two areas of production in which the Minoans were to excel throughout their civilisation. Galleries II and III cover the Old Palace Period, initially with more Vassiliki ware and small-scale sculptures from peak shrines (the Minoans were true miniaturists when it came to sculpture). There are also faience plaques depicting Minoan houses. The dominant pottery is now described as Kamares ware, much of it from Phaistos and the Phaistos area. Some Kamares vessels are perilously thin, and known accordingly as egg-shell ware. The Phaistos Disc is also exhibited here. This is a clay disc stamped in a spiral with hieroglyphics still impenetrable to scholars. It is sometimes claimed, at least half seriously, as an early example of printing.

Archaeological Museum, Irakleío: mosaic from Knossos detailing the Poseidon Chariot

Gallery IV is packed with Minoan artefacts of which some are magnificent and others tender and personal. It contains two tiny statues of priestesses, or perhaps goddesses, from the most sacred area of Knossos. One, with breasts bared, holds out snakes; the other, also bare-breasted, is liberally entwined with snakes. Here one may see the most famous Minoan bull's head, made of serpentine and with one surviving eye in jasper and rock crystal. It was probably a ritual container, called a *rhyton*, used for pouring out libations. A tiny ivory acrobat, caught in mid-air leap, shows how brilliantly Minoan artists could catch and convey movement and even portray such naturalistic detail as veins along an arm. There is a sword (from Mália) almost 3 feet (1m) long and a gold sword pommel, in the form of a disc with a hole in its centre. Another athlete is shown on the disc, bent right round backwards so that his feet rest on his head. Pottery masterpieces include a ravishing jug, covered all over with a pattern of reeds.

Cretan Axes

Irakleío museum contains many double-headed axes, either real or depicted on vast pottery storage jars. These axes were ornamental or symbolic, not for chopping or fighting.
In Greek the word for double-axe is *labrys*. Because the double-axe is omnipresent, it seems quite plausible that the word *labrys* was transmuted into *labyrinth* and used as the name for the palace of Knossos itself. This was a name which survived, and with great potency, into later Greek myth and almost every modern European language.

During the later periods, there were wonderful pottery vessels, often large, covered with writhing, flowing marine forms, the sad-eyed octopus the most impressive among them. From Agía Triáda (see page 31) come three carved conical *rhytons*, one showing boxing, one supposedly a chieftain receiving a tribute of hides, the third a procession of merrymakers. This latter, known as the Harvester Vase, is sometimes regarded as the finest low relief carving discovered anywhere in the Mediterranean basin. The Minoan sarcophagi in gallery XIII are a great surprise – bath-tubs used for burials and big clay chests called *larnakes*. The frescos just upstairs are marvellous, even though much ruined and much restored, often conjecturally. It is well to conserve some energy for them. The older ones are smaller than those made at the height of the New Palace period. They include a figure dubbed 'la Parisienne' at the time of her excavation. The face, with its huge eye and bumpy nose, the neck flowing with ringlets and with a sacred knot tied just behind, are remarkably vivid. There is the larger and newer 'Prince of the Lilies' with his plumed head-dress, a reconstruction which scholars have come to doubt, thinking now the original may have shown several figures. One of the most important exhibits in this room, indeed in the whole museum, is a painted sarcophagus from Agía Triáda. It is made of stone, and covered in painted plaster. This beautiful object clearly shows religious ceremonial in progress. In this gallery there is also the largest of the bull-leaping frescos, from Knossos, showing a male athlete, in mid-somersault. At the same moment a woman athlete begins her leap and another stands behind the bull to catch and steady the leapers.

The final rooms, devoted to the Minoans' successors, may come as something of an anticlimax; but they contain sculptures of great importance to the development of Greek art, and a set of bronze shields of immense beauty and significance.

AGÍA EKATERINI

Plateia Agía Ekaterini

This simple 15th-century church with a later Venetian doorway houses various fine works of Cretan religious art. The most beautiful are the paintings of Mikalis Damaskinos. Like his contemporary El Greco, Damaskinos also went to Italy, returning late in his life to Crete and here little by little re-adopting the 'Byzantine' ways of painting he had previously discarded. See particularly *The Divine Liturgy* and *The First Ecumenical Council* (1591), an unpromising-sounding subject for a marvellous painting.

Closed: Sunday.

HISTORICAL MUSEUM (ISTORIKO MOUSÍO)

opposite the Xenia hotel, west of the old harbour

This is more of a treat than many of its kind, containing displays that help to give some idea of Cretan life as well as Crete's tumultuous history. On the ground floor, there are portraits, weapons and other memorials of Cretan resistance fighters from Turkish times, the 'captains' or *palikares* whose deeds are also celebrated in monastery and schoolroom displays elsewhere in the island. There are religious objects, many from early days at St Titus in Gortyn and some notable icons (particularly pleasurable is the Zoodokos Pygi or 'Life-Giving Well'). The upper floors house a replica of the study of Cretan writer Nikos Kazantzakis (1883–1957, author of *Freedom and Death, Zorba the Greek*, etc) and celebrate Emmanuel Tsouderos, the Cretan who was Greek prime minister – and in refuge on Crete – during the battle for the island in 1941. He escaped over the White Mountains from Chaniá with King George of the Hellenes and was taken off by boat from the mouth of the Samaria Gorge. There is also an excellent collection of Cretan textiles and rural furniture and furnishings. This helps to enrich visits to villages in the Cretan countryside and is a particularly good preliminary for trips to the popular weaving centres of Anógia and Kritsá.

At various points in the museum there are illuminating photographic displays and in the basement there is a rich collection of architectural details and fragments.

Closed: Sunday.

KAZANTZAKIS TOMB (TAFOS TOU KAZANTZAKIS)

Martinengo Bastion

The epitaph for Kazantzakis's simple grave is taken from his own works: 'I hope for nothing; I fear nothing; I am free'. The tomb is set at the southern extreme of the Venetian walls.

VENETIAN FORTRESS (KÁSTRO KOULES)

at the end of the harbour mole

This large building, reconstructed in 1523, has been tidied and depersonalised in the process of contemporary restoration. But it is still impressive, with good views from the battlements and sundry

Crete's fortresses are a grim reminder of 400 years of Venetian rule

Lions of St Mark, the symbol of Venetian rule, carved in relief. This is the fortress that withstood the Turkish siege of 20 years and was finally surrendered by Francesco Morosini the younger in 1669. The siege was the last great stand of Christendom in the eastern Mediterranean. During the Battle for Crete in World War II the last Allied defenders of Irakleío fought their way along the mole and escaped to waiting ships. *Closed*: Sunday.

Accommodation

The traditional stopping-over place in Irakleío for the moderately well-heeled was for many years the A-class **Astoria** (tel: 081 229002). This hotel is right in Eleftherias Square, within whispering distance of the Archaeological Museum. Some of the rooms, especially on the upper floors, give pleasant views over the square; and though it may seem a little old-fashioned today, it remains popular and with friendly service. One or two more modern hotels have sprung up recently and some even offer swimming pools, most desirable in counteracting the hot and very 'towny' feel of Irakleío.

The **Galaxy** (A-class) in Dimokritias Street (tel: 081 232157) is one of the most promising, its rooms ranged round a central court with a swimming pool. The **Atrion** at 9 K Paleologou Street (tel: 081 229225) is B-class, and has the advantage of off-street parking in the town centre – a favourite of Greek businessmen. The **Daedalos**, C-class (tel: 081 224391) in pedestrian Daedalou Street, perhaps 100 yards/metres from the Astoria, is central, lively, and cheaper. There are youth hostels at 24 Handakos, and at 5 Vironos, between the bus station and Odhos Avgouston 25 (tel: 081 286281).

Nightlife

For Greek music, after 20.00hrs each night except Tuesdays, top spot is **Ligeros**, on the corner of August 25th and Epimenidou Street. There's dancing at one end and a fish taverna at the other. For Cretan music, and the sound of the plangent, three-stringed Cretan lyre – go to **Kastro** and **Delina**, on the way to the airport, convenient by taxi.

Restaurants

Nobody ever went to Irakleío for its restaurants but the dining situation is improving, particularly with the recently opened **3/4** (Tria Tetarta or Three-quarters), Theotocopoulou 1, a two-storey neoclassical building on the front. There are two bars, a café and restaurant, where you can eat good international food, if you can take your eyes off the fine sea views. There are numerous outdoor restaurants in Venizelou Square

Leisurely meals: a Cretan tradition

and a few in the narrow pedestrian street, Daedalou. The **Rover Pub** here is popular with tourists for its unthreatening cleanliness. **Aplo**, on nearby Milatou, is friendly and has live mucic. In a small alley leading between the market and Evans Street there is another press of restaurants, more ethnic and perhaps requiring a little daring for first-time visitors. These were originally the simplest of market restaurants serving great bowls of beans to villagers. Now they have turned to summer visitors as well and serve meat roast on the spit and over charcoal grills. Check prices first. There are also a few smarter restaurants, patronised by middle-class Greeks. **Knossos**, just round the corner from Daedalou, and **Kiriakos**, in Dimokritias Avenue, three minutes outside the city walls from Eleftherias Square.

Shopping

The market is the place to buy fruit, vegetables and oddments. Irakleío also has a full range of basic shops, many located in Kalokairinou, the stretch of main road between Nikephoras Phokas and the Chaniá Gate. These, however, are not remarkable. Smart boutiques, their presence an astonishment to those who have known Crete over the years, feature in Daedalou Street. There is a Christian Dior here, for instance, and smart Italian shoe and leather shops, fashionable clothes shops and Cretan art and artefacts of varying quality. Irakleío also has a few antique shops, though not all inspire confidence; try August 25th and K Paleologou Streets.

Agía Triáda has thrown up more questions than answers about Minoan life

WHAT ELSE TO SEE IN CENTRAL CRETE

◆◆◆
AGÍA TRIÁDA ✓

2 miles (3km) west of Phaistos
This set of ruins, excavated by the Italians and named after a nearby church (the Holy Trinity), occupies a site even lovelier than that of Phaistos (see below). On the western end of a hill, it looks across the final stretch of the Mesará towards the sea – which, in Minoan times, quite probably came right up to the foot of the hill. The mouth of the Kamares Cave on Mt Psiloreitis is also visible from here.

In general terms, Agía Triáda is a puzzle. What was the purpose of a set of secondary palatial buildings so close to the great palaces of Phaistos? It has often been described as a summer palace; it may have been used as a principal residence after the destruction of Phaistos; and there is also a suggestion that it may itself have been composed of two different establishments. For the non-technically minded visitor, the pleasure in this considerably less-visited site will probably lie mainly in its position and in the knowledge that many of the most beautiful of all Minoan works of art were found here. There was also a small township immediately adjacent, which included what looks remarkably like a row of shops. The conventional way to see the site is first to pay a visit to the small Byzantine chapel – Ágios Georgios Galatas, with 14th-century frescos – on a small hill opposite and slightly to the left. From here it becomes apparent that the palatial or semi-palatial buildings formed an L-shape. The splendid conical *rhyton* called the Chieftain's Cup was found among the small rooms just to the south (Archaeological Museum, Irakleio, gallery VII). There are a number of important rooms at the junction of the 'L', including one referred to as a hall, one with benches round its walls and restored gypsum cladding, and a third with a raised slab of gypsum in the floor. This may have served as a platform for a wooden bed. That great masterpiece the Harvester Vase was found in this corner of the site, along with the 'Boxer Rhyton'. They appear to have fallen through from the floor above – and smashed to pieces – at the time of the destruction of the building. In this area major frescos were discovered, including a marvellous scene of a cat hunting a pheasant (Archaeological Museum, gallery XIV). A little up right from these rooms, under a protective roof, there are chambers and magazines belonging to the main building. In Achaian times, a further palace appears to have been built on top. Outside, on the west side, run the remnants of a Minoan road.

The town and its shops, a dense, packed zone partly from the post-palace, Mycenean period lie further up, bending north-wards towards Psiloreitis to form a second L shape. The shops are in a row on the right-hand (eastern) side of the site. The beautiful and important Agía Triáda sarcophagus was found about 500 feet (150m) further east (Archaeological Museum, Irakleio gallery XIII).
Closed: Monday.

◆◆◆
GORTYN (GÓRTYS)
30 miles (48km) south of Irakleío on the main road to Phaistos
Sometimes known as Górtys (in direct transcription from Greek), this large and sprawling site is Dorian, Roman and early Byzantine. It has never been fully excavated and visitors may well find interesting ruins by wandering outside the peripheral fence. The most significant parts of the site, however, are enclosed within the fence.

It was on the banks of the river in Gortyn, so the Greeks believed, that Zeus seduced Europa, having taken the form of a bull, and brought her to Crete on his back. Europa, of course, has given her name to a continent. Historically speaking, the town rose to prominence only at the end of the Minoan era. It soon became an important city-state. An important pre-Roman remnant at Gortyn is the temple of **Apollo Pythios**, on the far side of the road. There is an altar and sundry bits of broken column. Roman Gortyn, which came next, was huge, with perhaps about 300,000 people. Unlike Knossos, it had sided with the Roman invaders in 65 BC and as

Laws of Gortyn

For us today, and especially for those interested in the law, Gortyn has a unique importance. Found among the later ruins – in which they had been incorporated as useful building materials – were a number of large, inscribed stone blocks. Reassembled and deciphered, these proved to contain the first known code of law in Europe, dating from the 5th century BC.

The laws of Gortyn are extremely hierarchical and match what is known of the conservatism and militarism of Dorian Crete. They deal, among other things, with property in marriage, and with adultery and rape. The code, which reads from left to right and then from right to left again, each line starting where the one before it ended, is beautifully incised.

a result was not destroyed. Instead, it became the capital of a province, controlling large areas of North Africa, and it possessed many impressive public buildings. The best preserved of these – just near the re-erected Code – is the

Stones at Gortyn: the ruins date from Dorian to Byzantine times

Odeum (1st century AD). This was a roofed building used for theatrical and other performances; there are fairly substantial remains. Possibly the most interesting building of all, however, is the early Christian **Basilica of St Titus**. Titus was sent to Crete by St Paul, who had himself had some adventures on the island. It was

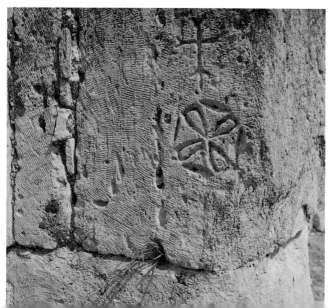

also Paul, in an epistle to Titus, who spoke of Cretans as 'liars, evil beasts, slow bellies'. Titus himself was martyred in Gortyn; the basilica supposedly marks the spot. It was a large building with triple nave and dome, bringing elements from Byzantium to an essentially Roman formula. A large and dignified section of the apse and its surrounds is still standing. Gortyn was sacked by Arab raiders in 825 AD and never rebuilt. But the Italian monk Buondelmonte, travelling in Crete in the 15th century, described its ruins as 'equal in grandeur to our own Florence'. The road leads on through Mires, a busy but rather ugly agricultural centre with numerous small restaurants, rooms to rent, and cafés for a cooling drink. It has a surprisingly energetic street life. A side road to the south leads to Mátala. Shortly beyond Mires, just off the main road, lie Phaistos and Agía Triáda.
Closed: Monday.

◆
HERSONISOS (CHERSÓNISOS)
17 miles (27km) east of Irakleío via the New Road
This is the first real resort as one travels eastward from Irakleío on the northern coastal plain. Technically its name is Limín Chersonísou – Port of Hersonisos. It is listed under 'L' in alphabetical publications (telephone book, official tourist literature, etc). Hersonisos has underwater relics of an ancient port and fish tanks cut into rock on the far side of the little headland. But for the rest, it is a modern creation (the original village is up and a little inland). The main road runs straight through the town. Beaches are in short supply but the front is prettily thronged with restaurants. Also on the front there are some surprisingly up-market boutiques, specialising in jewellery, leather and fur.

◆◆◆
KNOSSOS (KNOSÓS) ✓
3 miles (5km) southeast of Irakleío
Knossos is popular and crowded for the best of reasons: it is an extraordinarily interesting place. What stands out immediately is the extent to which it has been reconstructed. Whether or not the reconstruction is acceptable, the site certainly gives a strong impression of how a Minoan palace *may* have looked and makes subsequent visits to the other major palaces – Phaistos, Mália and Zákros – more rewarding.
With some small exceptions, what is visible on the site is the New Palace, built up after the earthquake of 1700 BC. The west wall is marked by the fire of its own final destruction in 1400 BC. Pathways crossing the paved areas immediately surrounding the palace are slightly raised, producing a 'causeway' effect. Entry is generally through the west porch and then along the wiggling remnants of the so-called Corridor of the Procession, parts of which have slipped off the corner of the hill. In due course one reaches an extremely handsome, pillared southern entrance where

KNOSÓS

1 Theatre Area
2 South Propylaeum
3 Throne Room
4 Pillar Crypts
5 Central Court
6 Priest King Fresco
7 Grand Staircase
8 Hall of the Double-Axes
9 Queen's Rooms
10 Shrine of the Double-Axes
11 Court of the Stone Spout
12 Pillar Hall

Digging at Knossos

The excavator and author of the Knossos reconstruction was the Englishman, Sir Arthur Evans. He began to dig just at the start of the 20th century at a time of high archaeological excitement. Over the previous 30 years or so the amateur archaeologist Heinrich Schliemann had been able to show, at Troy and sites on the Greek mainland, that there were substantial ruins at many of the places mentioned by Homer.

These antedated classical Greece by centuries. Schliemann had wanted to dig at Knossos but failed to buy the land. Arthur Evans eventually acquired the site, and years of major digs pushed back European prehistory by millennia, as they laid bare the bones of the foremost Minoan site.
Evans reconstructed as he went, in order to preserve his findings against damage from storms and earthquakes.

replicas of some of the major frescos are displayed (the originals are in the Irakleío Archaeological Museum, gallery XIV). The southern entrance leads to a large central court, a feature of all the principal Minoan palaces. An even more dramatic entry can be made through the narrow north entrance, though as you approach it you will have to pass several points of interest better left to the end of a visit (some well-like storage pits and a 'theatral area'). The northern entrance-way, achieving its present form late on, featured a narrow and steeply rising ramp passing beneath a porch which bore the awesome bas-relief of a bull (there is a replica in the proper position; the original is in the museum). This approach also leads into the central court. Here, on the westward side, there occurs a series of sacred chambers, dark and rather frightening. Deeper within is the throne room, where the throne, still on display, was found intact. On the eastern side of the court lay what appears to have been the domestic quarter. There was an upper storey here, but also several more below, cut into the side of the steep hill and reached by a wide and gently descending stairway bordered by colonnade and light-well and

Homer called Knossos 'a great city'; the palace ruins hint at past splendour

passing a series of fine rooms. Sir Arthur Evans named this the Grand Staircase and it is generally regarded as one of the most remarkable achievements of prehistoric architecture. Taking the stairway, the visitor first comes to a large fresco showing shields made of oxhide. Descending again, and turning to the right, one enters the Hall of the Colonnades. This in turn leads towards the so-called Hall of the Double-Axes, a name derived from mason's marks in the nearby light-well. It is also known as the King's Megaron. It was elaborately decorated and divided by a polythyron (a characteristically Minoan arrangement of partition with columns and door enabling a room to be shut off from wind and weather). Near by, reached by a narrow dogleg passage, is the room traditionally called the Queen's Drawing Room or Megaron. This fascinating room has a fresco of dolphins (the original is in Irakleío museum, gallery XIV). Near by is another chamber, bedroom or bathroom, containing a bath. There was also a lavatory with drains to carry away sewage. As well as the most spectacular parts of the palace, the 'theatral area' on the northwest corner of the complex is worth visiting. This really is just like a little outdoor theatre, with steps for a seated or standing audience. The Minoan road from the northwest leads straight up to it. Knossos is reached by a road leaving Eleftherias Square in a southerly direction or, for those coming along the coast, by a

turn off south from the New Road without having to go into Irakleío. Innumerable coach tours go to Knossos from Irakleío, not to mention the number 2 bus from Eleftherias Square. It is also easy to reach the site on day-trips from other resorts all along the north coast of Crete.

Closed: Monday.

◆◆
MÁLIA
22 miles (34km) east of Irakleío
Mália is one of the most extreme examples of tourist jerry-building in Crete, the brash and gaudy style of the resort contrasting sharply with the peace and beauty of the Minoan site a minute or two east by car. As at Hersonisos, the main road runs through town, with two good restaurants, the Taverna Plaka and the Melitos on either side at the far end. From the middle of the built-up area, a smaller road leads down towards the beach, so that shops, restaurants and discos are arranged on a T-shaped grid. Down at the bottom of the road is an excellent sandy beach which naturally gets rather crowded. Some have likened modern Mália to a frontier town on the Mexico/Texas border. But in all fairness it is probably good fun if you are under 18.

The Minoan **Palace of Mália**, one of the great four, lies just to the seaward side of the main road nearly 2 miles (3km) beyond the town. To the south in particular there is a fine mountain background, marking this as another brilliant choice of landscape by the Minoans. The ruins themselves, consisting as usual of fragments of the Old Palace and a lot more of the New, are relatively easy to understand, particularly if one is already a veteran of Knossos and Phaistos. There is the familiar arrangement around a central court – here a rather long and narrow one. The most sacred areas are to the west of the court and they are located close to storerooms. There are royal apartments, too, and part of the interest lies in seeing just where some of the most spectacular of the exhibits in the Irakleío Archaeological Museum were uncovered.

A raised causeway, typical of the Minoans, crosses the paved west court. At the southwest corner there is a series of circular storage pits, once roofed and most probably used for grain. Following the west flank and passing round the northwest corner, the visitor reaches the north court with giant storage jars (*pithoi*) on the left. To the right and slightly in front lie the 'royal apartments' with a lustral basin. The sword with acrobat curved round the pommel (Archaeological Museum, gallery IV), came from just west of here. On the nearer (northern) side of the Great Court was a pillared room, perhaps a kitchen with a dining room above, looking out over the court. As at Phaistos, the eastern side of the court was bounded by a colonnade in which stone piers alternated with upside-down wooden pillars. Various rooms found behind this to the east are now roofed and locked.

The most exciting area is the west of the Great Courtyard. Here there was a pillar crypt, probably dark and awesome as at Knossos, with double-axes scrawled into the pillars. A famous and much-illustrated axe-head in the shape of a leopard was found just near by, together with the great 'Mália sword' with rock crystal handle (both in gallery IV in the Archaeological Museum, Irakleío). The west side of the court had an upper storey and was undoubtedly imposing. At the southwest corner of the court is the most intriguing object of all, a round stone table with a depression at the centre and 34 smaller hollows round

the edge. Much ink has been spilled in trying to explain it. Ten minutes' walk from the site, northeast towards the sea, was the Khrysolakkos or 'Gold Hole', a burial place where the golden hornets of Malia and much other exquisite jewellery was found.
Closed: Monday.

◆
MÁTALA
55 miles (88km) southeast of Irakleio on Mesará Bay
This growing resort has a warren of man-made caves. They were occupied by hippies during the 1960s and gave the village a special reputation, somewhat unwelcome to locals. Nowadays the caves are closed

at night and Mátala has become a more ordinary little resort, very populous, and with a good but crowded beach and seafront tavernas. A rough scramble to the south leads past some decontrolled caves to a less frequented beach.
Mátala is reached by turning south off the main road in Mires, after Gortyn but before Phaistos, and passing through Petrokephali and Pitsidhia, 3 miles (5km) inland. It can also be reached by striking south from Agía Triáda.
Two other spots near by on the south coast may arouse curiosity. **Léntas**, reached by a turning just before Agía Déka, is not itself attractive – quite the reverse – but it has places to eat and sleep and there is a good beach 2 miles (3km) to the west. To the east of Léntas lie the remains of a Greek healing centre, or Asklepion, centred on what were once therapeutic springs. The Asklepion was also used during the Roman period.
Kaloí Liménes, reached via Mires on a moderate road, is spoiled as a resort by the presence of an oil-terminal on a small island opposite. Kaloí Liménes was the Biblical 'Fair Havens' where the ship carrying the prisoner Paul put in for shelter. Paul wanted to stay, but the centurion in charge of him joined forces with the ship's owner and they put out to sea – only to be engulfed by the tempestuous wind Euroclydon. They were driven on to Malta where the ship was wrecked.

Mátala's visitors once took to the caves; now they prefer the beach

FAISTÓS

Old Palace
New Palace

0   10   20   30 m

1 Theatre Area
2 Grand Staircase
3 Peristyle Court
4 Central Court

5 Queen's Megaron
6 King's Megaron
7 Treasury

◆◆◆
PHAISTOS (FAISTÓS) ✓

40 miles (64km) southwest of Irakleío between Mires and Tympáki

After Knossos, Phaistos is the greatest of the Minoan palaces. It shares many key characteristics with Knossos and visitors may find it helpful to have visited Knossos first. But for important reasons, a visit to Phaistos is a different experience.

While Knossos is rather dowdily placed on a low hill, Phaistos is on a knoll overlooking the verdant plain of the Mesará and then out over it to mountains. Southwards lies the smallish but attractive Asterousia range, separating the Mesará from the sea. Northwards, snow-clad for half the year, is the great sweep of Mt Psiloreitis, ancient Ida. (A distant blob of darkness high up on the mountain is the entrance to the sacred **Kamares Cave**, where worshippers left behind many examples of that fine pottery which is named after the cave.) The great beauty of the site, particularly in spring, is enough to persuade the visitor that the Minoans had a similar taste in landscape to ourselves. This feeling is reinforced by almost every other Minoan site except Knossos.

The second major difference is that Phaistos has not been reconstructed. The ruins, which are in fact extremely complex, seem at first sight simple and, by contrast with Knossos, pure. Phaistos was built originally round about 1900 BC, but, as with Knossos and the other palaces, the first structure was destroyed in about 1700 BC. A new palace was then erected on the site. Today a good deal of the Old Palace has been revealed by

excavation, and old and new are puzzlingly interlaced. The palace was excavated by an Italian team led by Federico Halbherr and Luigi Pernier. They started at the same time as Evans at Knossos, but publication of their findings came later, and therefore caused less stir.

Entry to Phaistos is across an open space usually called the Upper Court. From the southeast corner here a handsome staircase descends to the West Court, contemporary with the Old Palace. The court ended on its northern side in a wide series of steps, which remain beautiful and evocative. They must originally have been intended

Though not reconstructed, Phaistos gives a good idea of the palaces

as seating or standing space for ritual or performance, another 'theatral area' as at Knossos. Some archaeologists have speculated that bull-leaping sports, probably with some religious significance, took place here. From this position, it is easy to see the line of the front wall of the Old Palace, 23 feet (7m) in front of the New. Various areas roofed in with plastic lie to south and west. These are Minoan houses outside the palace walls, currently under excavation. Now the visitor climbs yet another set of stairs, extremely handsome and slightly sunken at either side to allow rainwater to run off. These lead up to the wide west entrance of the New Palace. This entrance changes almost at once into a warren of smaller divisions. Tucked away at a lower level are Old Palace storerooms – some with highly decorated *pithoi*.

Just to the right of the entrance in the New Palace complex were vestibules and guardrooms, a major set of storerooms and a room with lustral basin (in which ritual purifications may have taken place).

A few steps further south comes a series of rooms which were clearly associated with religious

At Phaistos the Minoan palaces looked out over the lovely Mesará Plain

worship, lying on the western side of the central court. This very fine courtyard was common to Old and New Palaces. In the time of the New Palace the buildings surrounding it probably stood two storeys high. North of the courtyard are the 'royal apartments'. These apartments offer nothing as spectacular as the Grand Staircase at Knossos and were not so elaborately painted. But they too have ingenious light-wells. The materials used for the finish were very fine and the total effect was probably more pleasing if less awesome. The finest had an alabaster floor, now restored, benches round the walls and alabaster dado. The so-called King's Megaron is of characteristically Minoan arrangement, with partition of piers and door. This part of the palace had its own lustral basin and, as at Knossos, there was an indoor, water-cleansed lavatory. The so-far unreadable Phaistos Disc, with its stamped spiral of tantalising hieroglyphics, was found among Old Palace buildings just to the east (now in the Irakleío Archaeological Museum). There is an acceptable café here too.
Open: daily.

Accommodation
The main interest in the coastal strip right along the north of Crete lies in the hotels and beaches, which often have a fine mountain backdrop. Moving west out of Irakleío there are various hotels – and beaches – almost immediately, notably the A-class **Creta Beach** at Amoudara (tel: 081 252302).

(For information about hotel gradings see **Accommodation** page 102.) This corner of coast, however, where the shoreline turns northwards, is entirely dominated by a power station. The New Road which rounds the cape leads to Agía Pelagía, a cove with sandy bay and a promontory. It has several hotels, principally the A-class **Capsis Beach** (tel: 081 811212). This large complex is set in gardens and has a good range of facilities, including tennis.
East from Irakleío, the New Road sets out along one of the strips of Cretan coast ravaged by uncoordinated tourist development. But even amid the mess there are some good hotels.
First after the airport comes Irakleío's municipal beach (pay on entry, showers). Shortly after is Amnisós, also effectively a town beach. Then comes Hani Kokkini, which has a number of hotels, among them the A-category **Arina Sands** (tel: 081 761113). There is a reasonable beach here together with a mass of new building in varying states of readiness.
Gouves follows soon, offering a strange peninsula of hotels, set apart from one another on a flat projection jutting out past a fenced-in US base. The most attractive hotel here is the **Grecotel Creta Sun** (tel: 0897 41103), A-category.
The luxury class **Creta Maris Hotel** at the western end of Hersonisos (tel: 0897 22115) is a good substantial hotel in the block-and-bungalow vernacular and with a pretty beach, the best in the immediate area.

RÉTHYMNO AND ITS PROVINCE

Réthymno and its broad strip of territory, reaching across Crete from coast to coast, commands delighted affection from its supporters. Though the 'nome', or prefecture, of Réthymno is very mountainous, it also seems welcoming and gentle. In the spring, especially in the high valleys, it is incomparably fresh and beautiful. The surprise is to find that its seemingly relaxed and gentle people have a history of independence, rebellion and self-sacrifice stronger than almost anywhere in the island. The eastern side of the prefecture consists of the mass of Mt Psiloreitis, which then drops away gently through high valleys with ancient Greek sites and Byzantine chapels. The land finally rises again towards the crags and peaks of the White Mountains in the west.

The centre falls away fairly steeply to the south, pierced by valleys and at least one respectable gorge, towards a coast of bay and beach set against a mountain backdrop and interrupted by massive headlands. The northern coast, by contrast, is flat and open, mostly fringed with sandy beach, and some of it has been developed most unattractively. Réthymno, at the centre of this coast, is a sleepy and delightful place out of season, and still seems sleepy even when busy with summer visitors. Its agreeable atmosphere makes a greater impression than its monuments, though one or two of these are striking.

◆◆◆ RÉTHYMNO ✓

Visitors entering the town from Irakleio will probably catch sight of the massive Venetian fortress, by far the most prominent feature of the town. Some little way after entry to the town, Kalergi V Street, to the right, gives access to the front, one possible point for starting a tour of Réthymno. Equally, visitors can carry on until they reach an open space, just before a walled park, to the left, and with a large new church immediately on the right. Beyond the church, also on the right but tucked away, a Venetian gate gives access down into the old town.

On the front, you will be confronted by the town beach, a long, busy hoop of sand backed by grass and backed again by the promenade or *paralia* which follows along the front in both directions. It is named **Eleftheriou Venizelou**, after Crete's great modern statesman. The tourist office, NTOG, is just to your right as you reach the front. The section of the *paralia* leading left towards the fortress is closed to traffic in the evenings. Along its landward side stands a row of old houses, once very handsome. Their upper storeys have been largely re-made in concrete, but their lower storeys often still survive in their original form, and incline outwards at the base as a support. These are now mostly hidden behind restaurant and cafeteria awnings.

Following onwards, keeping as close as possible to the sea, you will round the corner to reach the

Attractive old buildings line the busy inner harbour of Réthymno

very pleasant horseshoe of the inner harbour. Here similar old houses have survived without quite the same degree of reconstruction; these, too, are used as restaurants. Opposite are harbour sheds and, to the right, a pretty lighthouse. Beyond this a harbour mole extends out into the sea, sometimes with coastal steamers made fast alongside. A similar mole away to the right confines the eastern end of the town beach.

All this is effectively seaside Réthymno. Just behind it is a warren of lively little streets with interesting shops. The narrow little street from the southwest corner of the inner harbour leads past an old Venetian loggia, along Paleologou Street to **Petikhaki Square**.

One interesting route towards the square starts at the Venetian gate giving off the main road. The **Porta Guora**, as it is called, opens through a surviving fragment of Venetian town wall, leaving an isolated minaret away to the right. Ethnikis Antistaseos Street, the narrow road leading north from here to Petikhaki Square, is a real pleasure. It has everything from good bread and vegetable shops to Cretan crafts (see **Shopping**, page 47). Visible especially in the small streets leading off are stone-arched Venetian doorways and little boxed-in Turkish balconies made of ancient, sun-worn wood projecting at first floor level from even older houses. The road leaves, on its left, an old Venetian church converted into a mosque by the Turks.

In a moment, you have reached Petikhaki Square, converging with the route along the front. The square is nothing special architecturally, but it has eating places and a *kafeneion* (café). Beyond it is one of the most pleasing fountains of old Crete. This, the **Arimondi Fountain**, has lost its roof but still has Corinthian capitals and a lion's head as a spout. Beyond again is the great **Venetian fortress** and opposite its entrance the Archaeological Museum (see below). Sometime during a visit to Réthymno it is absolutely necessary to wander westwards from Petikhaki Square across the isthmus. The streets here are even more enchanting, with the same mixture of Venetian arches and Turkish balconies. There are various Turkish inscriptions, water-fountains, canaries hung out in cages, children scuffling about with footballs, carpenters

Shopping is not too hectic in charming Réthymno

unloading planks from small delivery vans in tiny streets – all the life of a little Greek town carrying on in parallel with tourist Crete. On the far side, the visitor will reach a larger square containing the administrative headquarters of the nome of Réthymno.
The rest of the town, inland from the main road, is expanding fast, with modest concrete blocks and modern apartments. There is the park and another mosque, by the bus station, with the remains of a third close to Eleftheriou Venizelou. Moreover, Réthymno has a great tradition of learning, and two of the faculties of the new University of Crete are here. So there are plenty of young people around – except, of course, during the summer vacation.

What to See in Réthymno Town

ARCHAEOLOGICAL MUSEUM
opposite entrance to the Venetian Fortress
This museum has good local exhibits attractively displayed; it proceeds mainly clockwise in chronological order. Good Neolithic material, early and middle Minoan material, late Minoan finds from Armeni (see also Archaeological Museum, Chaniá), and a notable collection of Greek and Roman coins make it worth a visit.
Closed: Monday.

NERANDZES MOSQUE
south of Petikhaki Square
This pleasing and delicate minaret is unfortunately closed for safety reasons.

THE VENETIAN FORTRESS
This was built in 1574, and fell easily to the Turks in 1645. It has huge ramparts and battlements, and good views over the town and coast. Within the perimeter, there are a church and a former mosque, empty official buildings and a sense of abandonment and loss. The fortress is on the tip of the promontory; the main gate is at its western end.

Nightlife
Réthymno has the ordinary run of discos plus one or two less usual venues, such as the bar-restaurant **Nikolao Gounaki** in Koronaiou Street, on the isthmus. Much hung about with Cretan 'junk', this dark dive features nightly performances on the Cretan lyre, and the singing of *mantinades*, the improvised rhyming couplets beloved of Cretans. There are more discos (including hotel discos) along the coastal strip to the east.

Accommodation
Most of the available accommodation in the area is to the east, along the coastal strip (see page 52). Travellers passing through will find a cluster of B-category hotels around the two adjacent bus stations.

Restaurants
Réthymno's best restaurants, or at least its fanciest, are those backing the Inner Harbour, with delicious smells of frying squid and fish, and tables grouped outdoors round the harbour. The **Taverna Vassilis** is attractive, with its masses of framed pictures, but **Mouragio Maria** and, really, all the others, are also worth a try. This little area gets crowded with parties visiting from elsewhere. There is a cheerful throng of less elaborate eating places round Petikhaki Square and the Arimondi Fountain, among them **Socrates 1**, **2**, and **3**! There is mass catering, with sometimes brusque service, under the awnings behind Eleftheriou Venizelou. Cafés on the *paralia* are enjoyed by younger people, with traditional *kafeneions* in Petikhaki Square.

Shopping
Réthymno is a town of some tradition, reflected in a scatter of craft shops. Nikos Leledaki, on the corner of Ethnikis Antistaseos and Souliou, supplies the villages around with traditional

RÉTHYMNO PROVINCE

Cretan leather boots, all hand-made and much-admired. Souliou, running from the southern end of Petikhaki Square to Paleologou, is a tiny street full of little shops selling good quality Cretan jewellery, leather, lace and cloth. Spiridakis at number 36 is one of several shops selling locally made lace and fine embroidered tablecloths, place mats and many smaller items. The Ware House Portalis, Ethnikis Antistaseos Street, and Emmanouela Markakys, by the bottom of Petikhaki Square, both sell traditional woven cloth.

RÉTHYMNO PROVINCE

After the New Road's holiday strip which follows the shoreline to the east, a flat coastal plain gives way to a rocky and indented coastline, mountains rising above, stony valleys leading inland, the road often some way back from the coast. The road passes behind capes with hidden cliffs and beaches to rise, finally, high above Agía Pelagía. This is the most exciting section of central Crete's north coast. There are no places of great note on the way, however – though some may like to explore the beaches of **Balí** (the best are furthest away along a side road doubling back towards the village).

There are two ways of travelling inland to Irakleío, cutting off the corner of coast round which the New Road runs; both ways, however, are much slower. The first possibility is to use the Irakleío Old Road running through the foothills via Pérama. This winds on through the villages of Mourtzaná, Drosiá, Damásta and Márathos, passes by the cone of Mt Stroumboulas and so to Irakleío.

Melidóni Cave (Melidóni Ántro)

When passing through Pérama, there is a possible turning 2½ miles (4km) to the left to the Melidóni Cave, which has been associated with the mythical giant Talos. He is said to have marched round the island keeping strangers off. During the insurrection against the Turks in the 1820s it became a mass grave for nearly 300 local people. After they had taken refuge here, their Turkish assailants blocked the mouth of the cave and then lit fires, asphyxiating those within.

The second route to Irakleío also starts off through Pérama but then, shortly after Mourtzaná, angles obliquely to the southeast, sweeping round in a shallow semi-circle to rejoin the Old Road again some 4 miles (7km) from Irakleío. This road winds up the northern flank of Psiloreitis, ascending through Garazó and Axós to Anógia before it drops down again. The place most people want to visit is Anógia – though the whole road is very scenic.

The coast road west traverses the plain, behind a shoreline of sandy beach. Until the vicinity of Georgiopolis and first views of the White Mountains it is actually quite a boring road. Excursions inland, however, will reward with glimpses of an older Crete. The road south climbs up towards Armeni, where late Minoan burials have been excavated in recent years. Seven miles (11km) later comes the first opportunity to turn right for Plakiás on a route which leads down through the Farángi Kotsifoú, the Kotsifoú Gorge. A mile (2km) later another possible descent leaves the main road, starting off through Koxaré, half a mile (1km) off the main road. This winds its way down through the increasingly spectacular Koutaliotiko Gorge. Do not be too alarmed even if you are arriving for the first time at night – others have got down safely before you.

What to See in Réthymno Province

The handsome monastery of Arkadi, once a guerilla stronghold, is a byword for heroism

♦♦♦
THE AMARI VALLEY

The south coast can be reached from Réthymno via the high Amari Valley, lying close in under Psiloreitis to the west. Take the road inland from Perivolia, just at the eastern edge of Réthymno, then up through Prasies and Filakio to Thrónos at the head of the valley. The road divides soon afterwards, the eastern side hugging the valley closely, the road to the west swinging away from it in places. This is some of the loveliest landscape in Crete; the area is rich in antiquities and Byzantine chapels. Not all are easily accessible and visitors intending to explore more fully may wish to consult a specialist guide book. At the southern end of the Amari Valley it is possible to turn east for Zarós, Agía Varvára and Irakleío or to continue south for Agía Galíni and the Mesará.

♦♦
ANÓGIA

22 miles (35km) southwest of Irakleío

Anógia is a mountain village with a bitter modern history. When General Kreipe, the German commander in Crete, was abducted by the resistance and taken off the island during World War II, Anógia was one of the villages which sheltered his captors – and, indeed, helped to hide General Kreipe. With the exception of the church, the village was destroyed in reprisal. Since the war, it has resurrected itself through weaving and handicrafts and, almost as soon as tourism began, established itself as *the* village for hosting parties for 'Cretan evenings'. And if some of the textiles insistently exhibited are less than wonderful, that is because tourists will buy them. All this being said, the village has a fine position, is alive and active and can be a very good place to stop, especially in winter.

It is also the starting point for excursions to the **Idaean Cave (Idaío Ántro)**, very high up on Psiloreitis. This may or may not have been the cave where Zeus was born (some plump for the Diktean Cave above the Lasíthiou Plateau) but it became a major place of pilgrimage for the classical Greek world. Pythagoras and the Cretan philosopher Epimenides paid it a joint visit. Today, the cave is fenced off to protect excavations in progress. For further details of the trail, ask locally or consult a guide book which contains routes for walkers.

◆◆◆
MONASTERY OF ARKADI (MONÍ ARKADÍOU) ✓

14 miles (23km) southeast of Réthymno
During the 19th century this monastery in the hills was at the centre of the Cretan independence movement, supporting resistance to the Turks. When Turkish assailants were on the point of breaching the walls during the rising of 1866, the defenders responded, so it is claimed, by putting a torch to their powder magazine. However it happened, there was certainly a mighty blast. Much of the building still stands – the powder magazine is roofless – but the force of the explosion killed hundreds of attackers and a great number of the men, women and children gathered within the monastery. The name of Arkadi was blazoned across the world, a code-word for heroism.

The monastery gate has been rebuilt. The church, somewhat pitted in places from the explosion, dates from 1587 and has one of the most decorative, and handsome, of all façades in Crete. The monastery has a small museum. A monument near by contains the skulls of some of those who died that day in November, 1866.

◆◆
AGÍA GALÍNI

on the south coast, southeast of Réthymno
Agía Galíni is the most popular and populous resort of the central part of the south coast of Crete. It occupies a narrow cranny of valley ending in a quarter circle of harbour with fishing boats and tourist boats, and a general sense of activity. The back end of the valley,

where the road enters, has been the scene of recent and prolific endeavours in concrete. You reach the sea by passing along busy little streets full of small restaurants and tourist shops. The front has a finished and settled air, with terraced 'rent rooms' establishments and tiny hotels climbing up a little rock face to the east. Every building on the front is a restaurant or café or tourist shop, or is hung with signs pointing on to yet another. Tamarisk, hibiscus and bougainvillea are all on show. It seems to be the very sense of confinement that the crowds enjoy – though in summer it is no place for claustrophobics. There is no listed hotel above B grade, a fact which gives some indication of the cheap and cheerful atmosphere.

Agía Galíni, once a small fishing port is now the south coast's most popular resort, attracting holiday-makers in droves

PLAKIÁS
on the road south from Réthymno, turn right 7 miles (11km) after Armeni
High and fissured mountains, grey in colour, rise behind this village. The coastal hills tip forward to form a semi-circular bay with Plakiás and its tiny harbour lying a little towards the west. The eastern end of the bay is closed off by a high crag. This is the prettiest setting of any coastal village in Crete, though it is not necessarily the friendliest place. One feels that development is arriving rather suddenly, perhaps disconcertingly. There is now a

group of package hotels on the front here with one or two outlying establishments to the east. Building is progressing apace along the one little road that runs back from the front. The stony beach stretching eastwards can be windy, and bathers often build themselves makeshift walls for shelter. There are discos and places to eat and have a coffee, and nothing very much more – but more will undoubtedly arrive. There are other striking villages behind Plakiás on the mountainside.

MONASTERY OF PRÉVELI (MONÍ PRÉVELI)

From Plakiás (see above) it is a short drive east, well in behind the coast, towards the monastery of Préveli. The road passes through a ravishing little valley, tender against its background of mountain. The turn down to Préveli passes a handsome 19th-century bridge, and then the very venerable ruins of the 16th-century monastic foundation out of which the present (17th-century) Préveli has grown. The road reaches the coast up above the beach from which Allied escapees from the Battle of Crete were taken off the island by submarine. A memorial tablet tells of 'the ferocious German reprisals' suffered by monks and villagers who 'fed, protected and helped' the hundreds of Allied troops. It then hooks round to reach the monastery, only the minimum of monks remaining. This important monastery reported directly to the Patriarch in Constantinople and became

extremely wealthy – a fact hard to believe today, given its isolated position.

Like Arkadi, the monastery was a source of continuous resistance to Turkish occupation and, like Arkadi, it participated in the 1866 rising. The tradition of independence was still alive at the time of World War II, when Préveli was used as a rallying point for Allied soldiers left behind after the Battle of Crete. A broad terrace with a splendid shade tree looks down over a slope with olives, cypresses and perhaps a grazing flock of sheep. The monastery church is 19th-century. Rules of dress are strictly applied.

Accommodation

The New Road towards Irakleío follows the shoreline east, leaving just enough room between itself and the sea for both the Old Road and a ribbon of tourist development, most dense from Plátanias on. This is a real mess, distressingly ugly, full of ill-assorted buildings, but lively even so. In the standard Cretan manner, several perfectly pleasant hotels and one particularly good one are located amid the mess. The good hotel is the A-category **Rithymna Beach Hotel** (tel: 0831 29491). With around 600 rooms, this is a community in itself. Despite a somewhat unfortunate khaki colour – quite common in contemporary Crete – it has all kinds of facilities, including supervised camping on the beach for children whose parents are staying in the hotel. The Rithymna Beach is very popular with families.

WESTERN CRETE

Western Crete has more capacity to astound than other parts of the island. Though not as high as Psiloreitis in the centre, the White Mountains (Lefká Óri) are far more awesome; the coast of the extreme west, despite magnificent beaches, is wild and little visited; the high rock wall of the southwest stands up out of the Libyan sea with impressive austerity. Most memorable of all, perhaps, the southern side of the White Mountains is cleft by the great **Gorge of Samaria** (see page 66). Though heavily walked, the gorge remains quite beautiful. Add to this Chaniá, reckoned by many to be the most vibrant and delightful of Crete's large towns; and add a people who are often dramatic, but open and friendly at the same time, and Western Crete offers a heady mix.

The Minoans were here in force, as we shall see, but their main places of habitation are still a mystery. Early and Classical Greek remains are remote and only enthusiasts will search them out – though some of the ruins are both impressive and wonderfully sited. There are Venetian monuments, a mass of Byzantine fresco painting, and Turkish minarets; and World War II cemeteries which many may wish to visit. But on the whole the visitor will probably spend more time with beach and landscape than on the cultural trail.

Most of the places to stay are in a coastal strip to the west of Chaniá, on the whole cheerful and enjoyed, but once again bearing signs of hasty and ill-coordinated assembly. From here, a proper visit to Chaniá is a must on any list. In addition, there are a variety of excursions to be made into the countryside and mountains, some in the course of a day, others taking longer.

Ancient Aptera near Soúda Bay was a powerful Greco-Roman city-state going back to the 7th century BC

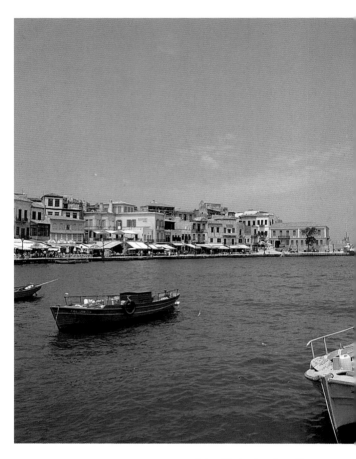

◆◆◆
CHANIÁ ✓

Of all Crete's major towns, it is Chaniá which has won the plaudits over the last 10 or 20 years. This popularity is due not so much to Chaniá's monuments as to its bracing position under the White Mountains, the thoroughly Cretan vigour of its inhabitants and the variety of its trades, from the manufacture of Cretan knee-boots to the carving of ornate and fairly dreadful furniture.

Much of modern Chaniá was destroyed by a firestorm during the Battle of Crete in 1941 and has since been rebuilt and enlarged. But in the old quarter round the harbour, narrow, handsome little streets survive,

Chaniá's harbour is a delightful place to explore

For at least two decades, Chaniá's old harbour has been recognised as the most attractive of all harboursides in Crete and the biggest single reason for the popularity of the city. At present, however, mass tourism combines with the continuing presence of Greek and American military bases on the Akrotíri peninsula to make things seem rather seedy here, particularly at night. Yet one would certainly wish to eat here at least once in a stay of any length, and one or two of the harbour-front lodging houses are most appealing (see **Accommodation**, page 59).

Platía 1866, the square at the top of Halidon Street, is one of the focal points of town, where the main road from Irakleio and Réthymno comes closest to the harbour. With its trees and shade and glimpses of the mountains, this square has a reasonable claim to being the centre of the city. It is the main stop for most city buses. The bus station proper is by its top end and the market, one of Chaniá's principal buildings, is just a little way back to the east. Halidon Street, not especially attractive in itself, is the main venue for fast food, quick-buy jewellery and tourist shops. Streets leading off it are the best place for leather (see **Shopping**, below). On the right of the street, towards the harbour, there is a paved open space with Chaniá's 19th-century **cathedral** at the back of it; an unexciting edifice. Here, in

many of them in the process of an improving facelift. Some are built into Venetian defensive walls. There is also an area of dignified neo-classical splendour from the period at the turn of the present century when Crete was an international protectorate with its capital here at Chaniá. The city remained the island's capital till 1971.

1770, the Cretan hero Ioannis Daskaloyiannis was flayed alive after surrendering himself to the Turks at the castle of Fragkokástelo in the south. Almost at once, to the left on Halidon, comes the door to the old church which houses Chaniá's **Archaeological Museum** (see page 59). Within just a few paces, the visitor will now reach a little open space known generally as **Harbour Square** (technically the **Platía Sindrivani**). Looking straight out across the water from the point of arrival on the front, there is a good view of one of the trademarks of Chaniá, the elegant **lighthouse** built by the Venetians and restored by the Egyptians during a brief period of control in the 1830s. Immediately to the right is a steep-sided hill, aptly named

Kastélli, the site first fortified by the Venetians and from which all later Chaniá has sprung. Parts of it are shored up still above the harbour by very old Venetian walls. On the left, the harbour front curves round in a half-circle of beautiful old buildings, the Akti Koundouriotou. Between the water and the raised bulk of Kastélli, there are two interesting free-standing buildings. The first is the Hotel Plaza, with a Venetian fountain tucked in just underneath its entrance. The second, the purpose-built but rather drab Mosque of the Janissaries, now houses a craft exhibition on one side and a restaurant/café on the other. Behind and carrying on round the corner to the right,

The Mosque of the Janissaries and Plaza hotel flank Chaniá harbour

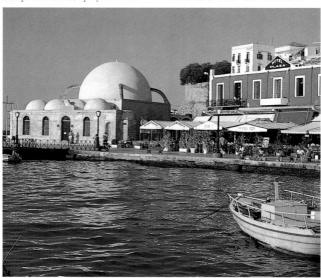

along a section of the front called Akti Tombazi, are more buildings of considerable age, restaurants and discos and eventually the shell of a large Venetian building now under reconstruction. Next comes a series of ruinous Venetian arsenals or warehouses. This last section of the front, lying along an inner harbour busy with fishing boats and yachts, is called Akti Enoseos.

Past the point where Halidon meets the outer harbour is the semi-circle of **Akti Koundouriotou**. Every one of the fine old houses here appears to have a restaurant, bar or café at its base, the awnings hiding much of the handsome architectural detail – steps, for example, mounting on a half arch up to a first-floor door. On the far corner of the hoop of harbour front, there is a **Naval Museum** (see below). Passing through the entrance here, you can reach the inner part of the **Firkas**, the Venetian fortification on the tip of this side of the bay. Here, in 1913, the Greek national flag was hoisted officially for the first time in Crete. The Akti Koundouriotou is the great tourist trap of Chaniá but one in which the visitor will want at some point to be caught. It is this area and the network of streets behind which sometimes seem a little threatening at night. Above and behind this part, however, there is a small area of great beauty and considerable antiquity. **Theotokopoulou Street** (named for El Greco) is its principal thoroughfare, running back from the sea along the top of the promontory with

fine old wrought-iron balconies and narrow alleyways leading off. One of the features of this part of town is the somewhat buried Venetian masonry of the **Renieri Gate**.

First-time visitors to Chaniá will probably want to begin by getting the feel of the harbour area and then radiate outwards. In this progression, Kastélli is the next place to visit – because it is near, because it is beautiful in its dilapidated way and because of the Minoan connection.

Chaniá was known to the ancient Greeks by the name of Kydoniá, and archaeologists increasingly suspect that Kydoniá may have become the principal settlement of Crete after the final destruction of Knossos. There is a strong presumption that there was a major Minoan palace here, perhaps on the Kastélli hill. No trace of it has yet been found, but a recent dig has uncovered parts of ancient Kydoniá. The site itself is not a palace but the finds are of palatial type; many are now in the museum. Perhaps the visitor is at this point standing very close to buried treasure of the most spectacular kind.

Kydoniá was a lively city-state during the classical Greek centuries, prospered under the Romans and continued to do well in the first Byzantine period. It later experienced a substantial period as the Venetian capital of Crete. Kastélli having been the site of the first fortifications, it is no surprise that Venetian memorials can be found on top among the decaying houses, lively now with younger visitors and pensions. Round the back of Kastélli, in Sifaka and Karaoli

Old buildings give the narrow back streets of Chaniá a timeless charm

Streets, there are interesting stretches where old walls and later houses are inextricably interlaced.

Beyond Kastélli one enters a part of town called Spiantza, with narrow streets, architectural oddities and churches which did duty as mosques during Turkish rule in Chaniá, from 1645 to 1898. Carrying on behind the coast one finally reaches **Halepa** – which is further than it seems and may justify the use of a car or a taxi. From 1898, during the period between the end of Turkish dominance and final union with Greece, Crete was first ruled by the Greek crown prince, under the eye of the Great Powers. The prince and his diplomats had their residences in Halepa and a little of this faded dignity endures. To the west from Halepa is Chaniá's main **market**, a large cruciform building, drawing a fine selection of produce, much from western Crete. The market is positively swollen with fish and vegetables, tobaccos and teas, strings of sausages and carcasses of goats and any other foodstuff you can buy in Crete. Its comparative order and sense of loftiness provide a strong contrast with the market of Irakleío and those who wish to linger may like to try one of the small restaurants among the stalls.

Across the road from the market, two rather more formal, European-type streets lead away southeast. These are Dimokratias and Tzanakakis, with Chaniá's large Public Gardens opening out between them some four blocks down from the market. Both have modern shops, airline offices, etc, and the latter leads to the **Historical Museum**. To either side, east and west, the modern city of Chaniá stretches out.

What to See in Chaniá

◆
ARCHAEOLOGICAL MUSEUM
21 Halidon Street
This is an old church, much beset by time but with an agreeable garden and appealing fountain. Exhibits, running roughly clockwise through time, feature most prominently a Minoan progression from western Crete, including important finds from Kastélli. In the centre are the fine tombs found in Armeni, near Réthymno. *Closed*: Sunday.

◆
HISTORICAL MUSEUM AND ARCHIVES
20 Sphakianakis Street, off end of Tzanakakis
An extensive collection portraying the island's folkloric history. Includes memorials of the statesman Venizelos, intimately associated with Chaniá, and of the struggle for independence which he brought at last to a successful conclusion. *Closed*: weekends.

◆
NAVAL MUSEUM
Akti Koundouriotou
Models, photographs and an interesting display of naval history.
Open: May to September.
Closed: Monday.

Accommodation
Most visitors stay on the holiday strip to the west of the city. In town, there is the A-class **Kydon** (tel: 0821 26190), just near the market, and several hotels around the bus station – the friendly **Samarias**, B-class (tel: 0821 51551); the **Omalos**, next door, C-class (tel: 0821 57171). On the front, if you can bear the throb of music, is the A-class **Amphora** (tel: 0821 42998), the prettiest building on the harbour, incorporating Venetian and Turkish elements and decorated with elegant simplicity. The prize for charm, though, goes to the B-class **Doma** at 124 Venizelou Street (tel: 0821 21772) just outside the main town. A neo-classical mansion separated from the front by a rather busy road but gracious within, stuffed full of antiques, old prints and Cretan fabrics.

Nightlife
The most favoured discos are **Ariadni**, to the right along the front, and the **Agora**, tucked into a corner of the market (around the east end of the building and up a flight of stairs). The **Fagotto** on Agelou Street features jazz bands and jazz piano. On Akti Enoseos, there is Greek dancing on the first floor of the bar **Pallas** and at **Cave Kriti** in one of the old arsenals, a chance to hear Cretan music and see local dancing.

Restaurants
Locals say the best fish restaurant in town is the unpretentious **Dino's** behind Akti Enoseos, the inner harbour. Dull brown décor but marvellous

squid, cuttlefish, prawns, octopus, etc, as well as straight-forward fish. Other good fish restaurants may be found near by – try **Karnayio** by the boats on Akti Enoseos – and on the front in the New Town, half a mile (1km) or so out west beyond the Naval Museum, try **Akroyiali**.
Inevitably one will also eat in the outer harbour – Greek style starters, fish and traditional Greek dishes. Just behind the outer harbour, Tamam on Zambeliou Street in the basement of an old Turkish building, is much praised by locals for good home cooking (evenings only). Round the corner off Kondilaki, **Marco Polo** is also recommended.

Shopping
Chaniá is one of the best places on the island for hand-made Cretan goods; and there is a concentration of craft shops in Ageiou, Theotokopouiou and Zambeliu Streets, behind the outer harbour.
For Cretan weaving, try **Kosta** at 5 Ageiou Street. He claims his collection of fabrics is between 50 and 130 years old and they are priced accordingly. The colours are rich and lovely, with varying degrees of elaboration in the weaving. Many of these items were made originally for dowries.
At 12 Zambeliu a tiny jewellery shop sells gold and silver jewellery in traditional and

Chaniá is a good place to look for exciting hand-made Cretan products

modern styles, with a little work-shop to the rear. At 81 Zambeliu are hand-made Cretan ceramics, including the work of two local potters. Soft blues are a speciality. Local handicraft producers have formed a co-operative to maintain quality; they have an exhibition in the Mosque of the Janissaries, with items for sale.

Back in Halidon Street, tourist knick-knacks and cheaper jewellery are on sale. Skridlof leading off to the right, as one descends, is the best place for leather goods. These can be very varied in quality. Smell the leather before you buy; if it smells rough here, it will smell worse at home. Belts, bags and lace can all be found in this area. (For the market, see page 58).

WHAT ELSE TO SEE IN WESTERN CRETE

◆
AKROTÍRI

The name Akrotíri means peninsula. The peninsula in question is the large, ear-shaped tract of land that juts up immediately northeast of Chaniá. The city's airport is roughly at its centre. Akrotíri is also a hot spot for military activity – whence the great number of military personnel taking their ease along with the tourists in Chaniá's bars and restaurants. The bases mean blank walls down on the flat and radar installations on mountain tops. In addition, Soúda Bay, bounded on the north by Akrotíri (see below), is the site of a major naval base regarded with great sensitivity by Greek security. The no-camera signs mean just that.

Despite all this, Akrotíri offers some notable modern history, fine beaches and several particularly interesting monasteries although new building threatens the landscape. The modern history is soon encountered. Where the Chaniá–Akrotíri road ends its climb up to the high neck of the peninsula, a turning left leads on to the hill of **Profitis Ilias** (the Prophet Elijah), with magnificent views back over Chaniá. In 1897, Cretan rebels raised the Greek flag on these heights and kept it flying despite bombardment by an international peace-keeping fleet.

Later, Eleftherios Venizelos, statesman and the architect of the island's unity with Greece, was buried here. The plainness of his grave (he is buried with his son Sophocles) makes an emphatic memorial. From here, the turning north leads on past Kalathas (two small beaches) to **Stavrós**, a notable circular bay and beach. The far side is bounded by a steep fall of mountain – familiar to many from the final scenes of the film version of *Zorba the Greek*. To visit Akrotíri's monasteries, take the right turn at Kounoupidiana, a mile (2km) along the main road past the Venizelos grave, then turn left as signposted 4 miles (6km) later (leaving the airport to southeast).

The first monastery is **Agiá Triádas**. This very handsome Venetian structure, founded in 1612 by a Venetian convert to Orthodoxy and pierced by one of the most grandiose entrances on Crete, has sonorous echoes despite its present decay. The

WESTERN CRETE

Monastery of Gouverneto's Renaissance-style church has an ornate façade of Venetian sculptures, and is a few miles further along a less impressive, though attractive, road. A few minutes further along again, now on foot, comes the **cave of** **St John the Hermit**, an important local saint, and finally, after about 45 minutes' walk in all, you reach the the long-abandoned **Monastery of Katholiko**, spectacularly positioned by a stone bridge crossing the bottom of a cleft.

A sun-drenched corner in one of the monasteries of the Akrotíri peninsula

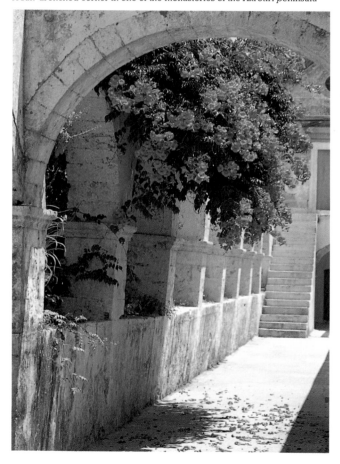

◆
GÁVDOS ISLAND

30 miles (48km) south of Sfákía

Gávdos is the biblical Clauda past which St Paul's vessel was driven on its way to shipwreck in Malta nearly 2,000 years ago. It is the largest and most southerly of Crete's island dependencies. Gávdos is interesting mainly because it is there; the people, though friendly, are few and not having an easy time, and the landscape is mild and unexciting compared to Crete. Even knowing this, one somehow has a strong urge to see it; and goodly numbers gratify that urge. The boat from Palaiochóra lands at Karabe. Then comes an hour's gradual climb on foot to Kastri, the village which serves as the island's capital. There are only a handful of families remaining here. For those visitors prepared to walk the several miles north or south, there is good swimming at the island's extremities. Water, however, is in short supply and food is limited.

◆
MÁLEME AND THE NORTHWEST

west of Chaniá

Máleme is reached on the main road west from Chaniá, some miles after Germany's memorial to its paratroopers – a diving eagle – and a strip of ragged tourist development. Máleme has long had a little airstrip. Shortly before Máleme's airstrip, a turning up to the left leads on to the former Hill 107, now the site of the German War Cemetery. Located just off the road leading up to the war cemetery, there is

> **Invasion at Máleme**
> To capture Crete in May 1941, General Karl Student, the German commander, needed to control, at a bare minimum, one of the island's north coast airstrips (the others were at Réthymno and Irakleío). At Máleme paratroops and gliders landed successfully, and during that night, the Allies retreated from the hill above the airstrip – 'Hill 107'. General Student opened up this weakness in the Allied wall, pouring men and munitions into Crete through the tiny airstrip of Máleme.

an elaborate Minoan tomb. Shortly, a road strikes off southwest to Palaiochóra – the route which most visitors take. But Crete's far west, even if relatively little visited, is a spectacular part of the island. Initially, the landscape is dominated by the two capes that stick up from the island's head like insect antennae. The first is Rodopou. At its base on the nearer or eastern side is the small town of **Kolimbari**, looking back towards Chaniá. There is an ancient monastery here with outstanding Byzantine icons and a modern seminary for Orthodox priests. Boats can be hired for trips north to **Diktýnna**, site of an important Greco-Roman temple, now thoroughly ruined.

Once across the high ground at the base of Rodopou, a wide view opens out across the Gulf of Kissámou to right, over the plain backing the town of Kastélli, and on beyond the gulf to the even wilder Gramvousa peninsula **Kastélli**, known as Kastélli

WESTERN CRETE

Kissámou, has an unemphatic ease, with a little scrap of square in the middle where passers-by can get a meal, more tavernas down on the front and the start of tourist development. There is a twice-weekly ferry to the island of Kythera and on to the Peloponnese. The plain behind Kastélli is rich in oranges and olives, and on a steep crag 4 miles (6km) to the south lie the ruins of the ancient city of Polyrhinnia.

Beyond again, towards the western coast and then a short way north, the ruins of an ancient port named **Phalasarna** can be found high and dry above the sea. The sands here are magnificent – but beware of oil on the beach. Southwards, a wonderfully rustic though sometimes alarming road – now being upgraded piecemeal – leads right down the whole of the far western coast (a distance of some 15 miles – 24km via the nunnery of **Chrysoskalítissa** to a point where it is possible to wade across the shallows to the shadeless but idyllic island of **Elafonísi**. In good weather, Elafonísi can also be reached by boat from Palaiochóra.

The whole of this western coast together with the roads and villages inland, must rank high among the most beautiful areas of Crete.

◆◆
PALAIOCHÓRA AND THE ROAD FROM CHANIÁ
The road west out of Chaniá turns south at Tavronítis to start its ascent via the large village of Voukoliés, a fruit and vegetable growing area, with an active

Saturday market. Climbing more steeply, with some fine views down over the Máleme coast and the Rodopou peninsula, the road eventually breasts a ridge and drops down into a wide and pleasingly contoured plain. All around there are churches with Byzantine frescos, some well-preserved, many ruinous, sometimes disfigured with a chalky film of white. The village of Anisaraki, on the Temenia road out of Kántanos, has no fewer than four Byzantine chapels; there are two at Kakodiki just on past Kántanos; and many, many more in the general vicinity. Shortly the road begins its descent to Palaiochóra. The dominant feature is a ruined

Venetian castle on a rocky outcrop, with the town tucked in behind across the isthmus.

As the main road comes into town it turns into a pretty little street, increasingly crammed with tourist shops and restaurants. These spill out to fill the whole street in the evening and traffic is diverted along the front, to the left. Here there is a pebble beach and sea-front restaurants, and a small harbour for local boats, including the south coast ferry. On the west of the isthmus, a long sandy beach backed by tamarisk trees provides some of the best bathing on Crete. It can be windy, though, and this makes it a leading spot for practised wind-surfers.

The south-coast ferry from Palaiochóra to Agía Roumeli puts in at Soúgia as a first stop. This little port and hamlet with a long beach has become something of a magnet for young travellers and will presumably evolve into a resort. It can also be reached overland from Chaniá and by a roundabout road from Palaiochóra via Kántanos. From Soúgia, it is possible to walk or take a village boat back just a little west to Lissós, an ancient Dorian settlement which survived into Greco-Roman times as a healing centre.

Church at Agía Roumeli, set against the backdrop of the hills of Samaria

◆◆◆
SAMARIA GORGE ✓
(FARÁNGI SAMARIÁS)

south of Chaniá
This is an excursion that many
will want to make, since the
gorge is extremely beautiful.
(Also see page 88.) However, in
high season so many others
make the trek that it is scarcely
possible to pause and look
upwards at the splendours.
The descent of the gorge is a
long 10 miles (16km), hard on
the legs and knees and
demanding good footwear. The
gorge is open only from May to
October because of the fierce
flash-flooding that can occur,
sometimes with fatal
consequences. So, though
Samaria is an extremely popular
hike, it is also an undertaking
(allow 5 to 6 hours).
Chaniá is the nearest starting
point, but the excursion can be
made by coach from many other
tourist centres. The most
enjoyable tours are those which
start from the nearer resorts,
reach the gorge early and allow
walkers to make the descent
before it gets too hot. The further
away you start, the hotter and
wearier you will be by the end.
Samaria-bound buses first make
their way up and up to the
pancake-flat, mountain-ringed
plain of Omalós, a word meaning
belly-button. This plain,
regarded by at least some of the
ancient Greeks as the navel of
the world, was the scene of a
famous meeting of rebel leaders
during the Cretan revolt of 1866.
It is celebrated in a folksong
which was often performed as a
gesture of defiance in nightclubs
and other places of
entertainment under the
dictatorship of the Greek
Colonels during the 1970s. The
buses decant their passengers
near a useful drinks stall. Those
doing the walk then begin an
immediate descent, with a
thrilling rock face opposite,
down a well-built zig-zag path
called the Xyloskalo, or Wooden
Stairs. The path drops through
perhaps 1,000 feet (300m) in
half a mile (1km), amid the fresh
smell of cypresses, glimpses of
the rock face opposite and with
a pocket of blue sky above. It is
advisable to take refreshments,
but there are several springs,
and some may want to carry
bottles and fill them at the
springs. The route levels out
when it joins the stream bed at
the bottom of the valley. But the
going gets rough underfoot, with
only loose rocks to walk on now
for most of the remainder of the
journey. If you can manage to
look up, you will see trees
clinging crazily to the cliffs
above, birds wheeling and,
always, a sense of grandeur and
loftiness.
Walkers soon come across a
little church, and then the
abandoned village of **Samaria**,
on the far side of the stream
rather less than halfway through
the walk. There is a public toilet
and plenty of people picnic on
the grass round about. Then
comes another little church, and,
after a long interval, the walker
arrives at the Iron Gates, or
Sideresportes. This is the point
where the high rock walls of the
gorge narrow to about 15 feet
(5m), with the stream,
sometimes a flood, tumbling

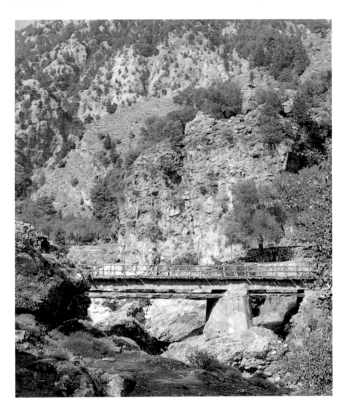

Only fit walkers should attempt a hike through the Samaria Gorge

between them. It is the high point of the gorge experience. After this, a fairly long stretch leads on to **Old Agía Roumeli**, a semi-abandoned village with several pretty peasant court-yards and two small shops selling drinks and postcards. This is followed by a hot and dull final stretch across a diffuse stony terrain to the modern settlement of **Agía Roumeli**. Considering that it has no road, this little place has become astonishingly active, with masses of building and cement and a harbour in process of construc-tion at the west end of the shingle beach. The beach itself shelves sharply so that within a step or two the deliciously cool water is bearing the weight of the weary walker. There are meals and drinks to be had here in plenty. At the appointed hour, with any luck, the boat service will ferry you on to Hora Sfakion. This is a fine boat-ride under an imposing coast, with a possible stop in **Loutró**, a tiny semi-circle of village backing an almost perfectly round bay. Loutró is accessible only by boat or on foot and remains one of the most charming places on Crete. It is also possible to make the Samaria walk on trips starting in Palaiochóra to the west. There is a boat service via Soúgia back to Palaiochóra. The journey west is tremendous, the ferry feeling perilously small under great falls of cliff. What appears to be a waterline some way up on the cliff face is precisely that; the southwest coast of Crete has risen by approximately 26 feet (8m) since classical antiquity.

Loutró, accessible only from the cliffs or the sea, is a gem

SFÁKÍA
southeast of Chaniá on the south coast of the island
The high, bare landscapes of Sfákía are somewhat dispirited today and badly depopulated but, Minoan sites aside, this is the most celebrated region in the island. With its capital at Hora Sfakion and its territory running from the island's backbone down to the south coast, Sfákía is famous for a long list of attributes. First comes its past ferocity, expressed as heroism or brigandage depending on circumstances, but traditionally combined with intense loyalty to its own people. Then there was its sense of independence, extreme even for Crete. Sfákía was also known for huge and bombastic boastfulness; and for

the deep, rich seams of folklore which have helped give it so strong a sense of itself.

It probably derived much of its character from centuries of isolation behind its mountain barrier. Writers from the 17th century onwards describe the Sfákiots in the most vivid terms. All males bore arms – this was true up to World War II and beyond. They practised the vendetta and bride-stealing, they believed in vampires, and men and women alike were tremendous dancers. The Sfákiots were the originators of many serious revolts against the Turks – disregarding the retribution wreaked on the lowlanders – and they themselves frequently raided the lowlands. During World War II, the Sfákiots behaved with the courage and dignity that might have been expected from the more serious side of their legend, first sheltering the Allied troops left behind after the Battle of Crete and then taking an important role in the resistance. The road south from Vrýses, a pleasant village south of the New Road, about 20 miles (30km) southeast of Chaniá, soon begins to climb towards Sfákia. The church of the Panagía in **Alíkampos**, a left turn 3 miles (5km) from Vrýses, has fine 14th-century frescos by Ioannis Pagomenos. He was one of only a few painters to sign his work, which is surprisingly prolific in western Crete.

Back on the main road, the traveller is following the route taken by the Allied Army during May 1941, on their desperate retreat.

Having climbed to a considerable altitude, the road crosses the plain of Askifou, passing the village of Ammoudároi and, further on, Ímpros. From here, it is possible to walk down towards the coast inside the fine Ímpros ravine. After Ímpros, the road itself soon comes out on to open slopes, with wide views beneath and a sense of exposure, as you track your way down through hairpin bends. At the bottom, turn right for Hora Sfakion, and left for Fragkokástelo.

Hora Sfakion (often simply called Sfákia) will not detain the visitor for long. Once Sfákia had its own fleet and the town was famous for the number of its churches. Now it is a nonentity of a place, with tavernas and rooms to rent and a waterfront plaque to commemorate the evacuation of troops by the British navy in May 1941.

From the port of Hora Sfakion, boats leave for the bottom of the **Samaria Gorge**, and, more importantly, the boats bring back to Sfákia the many walkers who have already descended through the gorge with organised tours. These tours commence in the plain of Omalós in the centre of the massif (see page 66).

A road uphill to the west leads to the substantial Sfakiot village of **Anópoli** on a high plain under the White Mountains.

Returning eastwards along the coast and passing the point where the main road comes in from Vrýses, the first major event is the Venetian castle of **Fragkokástelo**. This splendid honey-coloured castle, visible

WESTERN CRETE

Anópoli
Anópoli was the home of Ioannis Daskaloyiannis, the greatest Sfákiot hero of all – memory of him lives on partly because his deeds are the subject of a Cretan verse epic. Egged on by agents of Catherine the Great of Russia, Daskaloyiannis raised the flag against Turkey in 1770. He eventually surrendered after the capture of his brother and was ultimately tortured to death in the cathedral square in Chaniá. Turkish reprisals broke the power of Sfákia, which has never since recovered.

---

on the right and reached most easily by the second of the turnings which lead down to it, is nothing more than a shell. In 1828, during the War of Independence, the mainland Greek leader Hadsi Mikali Daliani took up position here and rashly met the Turks in open battle. He and his troops were annihilated, but there is a local legend that their ghosts can still be seen in springtime on the anniversary of the battle. They are called the Dhrosoulites, or Dew Shadows.

◆
SOÚDA
east of Chaniá by the Old Road
This long deep-water inlet, with a fortified island at its mouth and Akrotíri to the north, has for many centuries been the main anchorage and the centre of naval power on Crete, just as it is today. The large and poignant Allied War Cemetery is at the base of the bay, and then comes

Soúda itself, a drably functional little place with adequate facilities for passengers arriving and departing on the Piraeus ferries. New Road and Old Road merge here, and after the merging of routes, the road sweeps along the south coast of Soúda Bay. There is a large-scale Venetian fortification at Kalámi, and a spectacular view of Soúda Bay for those coming in the opposite direction. Mid-way across the water, the fortifications of Soúda Island look misleadingly like something out of toytown. The island in fact held out against the Turks for nearly 50 years after the fall of Irakleio.

Accommodation
Most accommodation in western Crete is to be found in Chaniá (see page 59) or along the coastal strip to its west.
The **Chandris Crete** (tel: 0821 62221) is a large A-category hotel set just behind the beach in Máleme. There are several modest but acceptable hotels in Palaiochóra, as well as smaller B- and C-class hotels in Agía Marína, Plátanias, and Kastélli Kissámou (Kastélli).

Ágios Nikólaos

EASTERN CRETE

In Ágios Nikólaos, eastern Crete possesses the island's best known resort. Though this is a pretty place, deserving its mild celebrity status, there is more to be found in eastern Crete. Compared to the Chaniá region, the east end of the island is almost gentle in its scenery; but it is still more rugged than, say, Corfu or Rhodes, and its villages often reflect an old and thoroughly Cretan lifestyle. The entry to eastern Crete – the prefecture of Lasíthiou – leaves the Dikte mountain range to the right. Then comes the outstanding Gulf of Mirabello (Mirampéllou), with Ágios Nikólaos on its nearer side

Old chapel against the backcloth of historic Soúda Bay, a restful spot away from the tourist trail

along with much smaller but more up-market **Eloúnta**. The famous island of Spinalógka is just off Eloúnta, while 6 miles (10km) south of Ágios Nikólaos the hill village of Kritsá offers the best of Cretan weaving, a stunning Byzantine church and a side-trip to a set of ruggedly dramatic Dorian remains. Past Ágios Nikólaos, and roughly following the north coast, one of the most beautiful of all the island's roads leads to the sleepy town of Siteía, technically Crete's fourth city after Irakleío, Chaniá and Réthymno. Siteía is in fact less of a centre these days than Ágios Nikólaos and has few monuments or special points of interest, but it is agreeable in its atmosphere and could well be worth a stay. From here, one can go vaulting onwards to the furthest east, to Vái with its indigenous but over-rated palm-grove and to Káto Zákros, extremely remote but nevertheless the site of the fourth great Minoan palace. This whole eastern end of Crete is rich in Minoan sites and has contributed many items to the Archaeological Museum of Irakleío and the museum at Ágios Nikólaos.

The resort of **Ierápetra** on the southern coast is a place much visited by package-tourists. It may be reached from Ágios Nikólaos, by following the Gulf of Mirabello and then striking due south; or by travelling diagonally southwest from Siteía. There are interesting places to see on these routes, but Ierápetra itself is not particularly rewarding. It is a medium-sized town of little charm, but it does have a long beach and a good winter climate, and package holiday hotels are thick on the ground.

◆◆◆
ÁGIOS NIKÓLAOS ✓

One of the great delights of Ágios Nikólaos is the first glimpse of the feature that has made the town its fortune, the small deep-water lake at its heart, enclosed by dramatic cliffs and linked to the sea by a narrow artificial channel. The little bridge across this channel, joining the two parts of the front, is the epicentre of Ágios Nikólaos. Around this hub, and the cheerful port on the seaward side, there has grown up a newish town, which is very busy in the tourist season.

The journey from Mália to Ágios Nikólaos is short and quick. As it follows the last stretch of the north coast strip, the Old Road gives access to one or two seaside places like Sisi and Mílatos, still fairly out-of-the-way but destined, it would seem, to achieve resort status. Then both Old and New Roads turn inland and climb over a mountain ridge before descending past **Néapoli**.

Traditional ways continue: washing wool near Ágios Nikólaos

This fair-sized town was the administrative centre of the prefecture of Lasíthiou until recent years, a role which has now passed to Ágios Nikólaos. At Dríros, very near Néapoli, there are remains of an important Greek temple. There is also a road due east, which descends steeply and through many bends to Eloúnta, offering magnificent views of the Gulf of Mirabello and the mountains rising beyond. The main road runs down southeast from Néapoli to Ágios Nikólaos. In Ágios Nikólaos itself, the front consists mainly of hotels. Around the harbour, there are shops, restaurants and discos, with cafés densely packed on the southeast side of the deep-water lake, **Lake Voulísmeni**. Two roads with tourist shops and boutiques – 28 Octovríou (October) Street and Koundourou Roussou – lead up to a little square with greenery, called **Platía Venizelou**. The only other street of particular interest is **Sfakianaki**, which cuts across from the harbour front to a small bay on the eastern side of the town. The bay is called **Kitroplateia**, perhaps because citrus fruit (*kitro*) was handled here. Today, its rocky shore is used for swimming. There is a (paying) municipal beach on the south side of town past the bus station and a slightly better beach a mile (2km) farther on. In terms of swimming, however, Ágios Nikólaos is a poor prospect and holidaymakers in search of beaches will do well to get out of town during the heat of the day.

What to See in Ágios Nikólaos

ARCHAEOLOGICAL MUSEUM

Konstandinou Palaiologou Street
This museum, past the lake on the seaward side, is Crete's most important archaeological museum after Irakleío, with a remarkable and growing collection. Exhibits, exclusively from the east end of the island, are pleasantly housed in a modern building more attractive from inside than out. Many digs have taken place in the east during the past 20 years and the pace of discovery remains rapid. As with Irakleío, some of the pleasure lies in linking particularly important or beautiful finds with their places of discovery, either visited already or on one's list of intended excursions. Items on display include a collection of grave-goods from over 250 graves at Agía Fotiá, beyond Siteía; and a collection of bronze daggers, one of them carefully bent over double like a folded tongue to render it harmless for the after-life.
Mýrtos, west of Ierápetra in the south, has contributed an extraordinary Early Minoan

'goddess', regarded as a masterpiece but looking, to a non-specialist, somewhat bizarre. The goddess is a bell-shaped pottery figure, with clay lumps for breasts, a triangle of pubic hair painted like a fish-net and a jug cradled in her arm.
There are many examples of Vassiliki ware, that odd mottled pottery already noticed in the Irakleío museum. The most characteristic shape resembles a teapot with an elongated spout. The loveliest things of all, perhaps, come from Móchlos, up on the northeast corner of the Gulf of Mirabello. The original finds here at the start of the present century included stone-jars of Early Minoan II and III periods, among the most glorious objects in the Irakleío museum. The museum has a wide range of Middle Minoan figurines from a number of peak sanctuaries and these, though highly simplified, demonstrate once again the Minoan gift for naturalism and the capture of the passing moment. It is fair to say, though, that the museum is a disappointment for the New Palace period – the best material from Zákros is, after all, in Irakleío. The display concludes interestingly with various exhibits ranging from an ivory crocodile to fine Daidalic sculpture.
Closed: Monday.

Nightlife

Young people give top rating to **Studio Disco** on the front. **Lipstick**, a not dissimilar establishment, is two buildings along. For spectacular views at dawn, try the all-night **Cafeteria Bar Yachting Club**, out on the harbour mole.

Restaurants

There is a plethora of restaurants in Ágios Nikólaos and prices are generally higher than elsewhere in Crete.

The **Cretan Restaurant** on the front (turn right at the bridge) is lavishly decorated with pot plants, textiles and stuffed birds and gets good reports even from locals. The **Trata** in Sfakianaki Street is a smartened-up taverna, and the **Ítanos** on a side street going uphill from Venizelos Square is closer to the real thing. Get good Greek food at **Posidon**, Soph Venizelou 26, running down to the bus station. **Synantisi**, 55 yards (50m) from the main crossroads to Eloúnta on the northern edge of town, offers good food and village wine away from the tourist hubbub. There are other eating places along the waterside just north of the town.

For an aperitif, the prettiest spot is the traditional-style ouzo bar, or *ouzeri*, **O Vios Einai Oneiron**, translated on a signboard as 'Life is Beautiful'; on the corner of Pasifais and M Sfakianaki. Design and woodwork are by the owner, the woman architect and carpenter Maro Dayiantis. There are delicious small eats to go with drinks, which can be taken either in the courtyard or in a pastel-painted sitting room with lace curtains billowing at the windows when the north wind, the *meltemi* blows.

Beer bars and fast-food joints abound in Odhos 25 Martiou, (25 March Street) running off Sfakianaki one street behind Koundourou. George Koumakis's **Asteria Café** just by the bridge occupies a fortunate position; and local high school students, knowing a good thing, hang out at **To Kafeneion** (The Café), an eagle's nest above the lake on Nik Plastira Street.

Tourists and locals alike enjoy the relaxation of café life in Ágios Nikólaos

Shopping

Ágios Nikólaos has a range of quite smart shops, selling mainly jewellery and furs, intended to cater for shopping as a holiday pastime. The more expensive shops are closest to the harbour. Underneath Rififi, on the harbour corner of Koundourou Roussou, L Maris sells both traditional Cretan designs and modern gold jewellery. The gold, as often on Crete, is bright yellow. Sofia, at number 33 sells old Cretan jewellery, clothes and rugs. Going up the road away from the harbour there is an excellent bookshop, leather and expensive fur shops as well as tourist knick-knacks.

In a short side-street joining Koundourou Roussou and Oktovriou 28 Streets, the dress designer Maria Patsaki has a two-floor shop. The ground floor contains displays of Cretan ceramics and jewellery. Upstairs, there is an interesting collection of traditional Cretan clothing, old and new,as well as a range of rugs, fabrics and much more.

WHAT ELSE TO SEE IN EASTERN CRETE

◆◆◆
GOURNIÁ

at the southern end of the Gulf of Mirabello

The Minoan town of Gourniá lies a short way behind the sea, climbing up out of a little valley on to a knoll. At the top of the knoll, there was once a complex of larger buildings, not palatial but probably occupied by people of standing or authority.

There are remains of a public courtyard here and a small courtyard inside the 'official' buildings. For the rest, the township is made up of a warren of tiny lanes, stepped and cobbled and big enough only for a laden donkey. The small basements and semi-basements undoubtedly had one more storey on top – the evidence for this lies in the stone steps which the visitor will notice. Various artisan dwellings have been found here, so that our impression is of a small manufacturing town of 1450 to 1550 BC.

Closed: Monday.

◆
ÍTANOS AND VÁI

far eastern coast

Vái has a fine beach and a grove of palms of a kind peculiar to Crete, producing inedible dates. It also has masses of visitors, lured by exaggerated tales of the palm grove, and the beach gets packed. Ítanos, a little further north, has fewer people and the remains of a once-important city-state. Dropping south from Vái and Ítanos, there is an important Minoan site at **Palaíkastro** which will interest mainly the specialist; and there are one or two places to stay.

◆◆
KRITSÁ

7 miles (11km) southwest of Ágios Nikólaos

Kritsá is a substantial hill village, much frequented by day-visitors and bus-tours. It is on the whole attractive, despite the tide of visitors, lured by the local weaving. Good quality Cretan cloth and articles made up from it are manufactured here and sold, generally at a better price than in the towns. Leather goods are also plentiful.

◆◆◆
THE LASÍTHIOU PLATEAU
southwest of Ágios Nikólaos
This is the largest of Crete's high, flat valleys and one of the most remarkable geological formations on the island. It is drained by a swallow-hole in winter and irrigated in summer by small, canvas-sailed windmills (assisted nowadays by many petrol-driven pumps). The famous cave which may have been regarded by the ancients as the birthplace of Zeus is a few minutes' walk from the plateau.

Though too high for grapes or olives, Lasíthiou is a major agricultural area, specialising in potatoes, apples and cereal crops. Because it was ringed by a protective mountain rim, Lasíthiou was often a centre of revolt. In order to put a stop to this, the Venetians banned agriculture here for some 200 years – even though they badly needed the grain.

The main village in Lasíthiou is Tzermiado. The **Diktean Cave** (Diktaío Ántro) is reached from Psihro, either by walking or on a donkey. The cave was a major centre of pilgrimage for about 1,000 years from Middle Minoan times onwards. There are routes up to Lasíthiou from Metohi, Hersonisos and Mália on the north coast, from Néapoli and from Ágios Nikólaos. All have their own beauties and surprises.

The church above the village of Tzermiado in the Lasíthiou Plateau has fine views of the Díkti Mountains

EASTERN CRETE

◆◆◆
LATÓ

2 miles (3km) from Kritsá

At the entry to Kritsá, a dirt road leads off right to Lató, a Dorian site perching on a high and rocky saddle. It boasts an acropolis at either end, and magnificent views down to the coast and back up to the Dikte Mountains. The ruins are massively solid, with a theatre and temple close to the normal point of entry. The saddle features a shrine, a rock-cut cistern and a set of steps rising beyond the courtyard in a manner reminiscent of Minoan theatral areas. The original entry to the city is down a walled and stepped alleyway to the left (it is in fact possible to reach this entry first of all by a lesser used and rather rough road, left instead of right at the final divide before the ruins). Above the flight of 'theatral steps' rising beyond the courtyard there is more evidence of massive building, some on fearsomely steep ground. In Lató, one has the sense of a people conducting an elaborate religious and cultural life behind the most rugged of fortifications. This is impressive enough – but it is the position which impresses most.

◆◆◆
MONASTERY OF TÓPLOU (MONI TÓPLOU)

11 miles (18km) east of Siteía

This famous fortified monastery, now refurbished, is reached by the coastal road from Siteía. It has strongly defensive outer walls and a pleasing inner courtyard, with the abbot's quarters and cells on several levels. There is a well known inscription here, part of the judgement pronounced in a border dispute between ancient Greek city-states in eastern Crete. There is also an 18th-century icon in the church, regarded as a masterpiece. This illustrates the prayer beginning 'Lord, thou art great' and contains 61 tiny scenes, all full of detail.

◆◆◆
THE PANAGÍA KERA ✓

Just east of the village of Kritsá (see page 76) stands one of the most beautiful churches in Crete, the Panagía Kera (Our Lady of Kera). Though neither large nor grand, this whitewashed building set among cypresses contains within its immemorial walls the most complete and best-preserved Byzantine frescos on the island. It takes a surprisingly long time to work them out, but patience will be rewarded. It may also be helpful to buy a copy of Emmanuel Bourboudakis's pamphlet on sale at the church. The Panagía Kera has three naves. The paintings in the central nave are the oldest, done in two different stages during the 14th century. There are gospel

scenes in the dome and on the vaulted roof of the nave – note particularly Herod's Feast and the Last Supper. Herod's soldiers are a tough-looking lot, contrasting with the elegance of the Venetian tableware in the picture. In the north aisle, the Second Coming is impressive, with its many haloed saints. There is a joint portrait of the church's founder and his wife. Both these aisles also have notably grotesque scenes concerned with the punishment of sinners. The south aisle, the first you enter, is the brightest and offers a display of human emotions to which we can still respond. The pictures here tell the story of Mary's mother Anne and of Mary, showing her pregnancy and Joseph's sorrowful reaction. The experience of the church, if one can find the time and curiosity to make the most of it, is both powerful and intimate.

◆◆
SITEÍA

43 miles (69km) east of Ágios Nikólaos

Siteía lies in an L-shape at the base of its own bay. The corner of the L is the central point, the Plateia Venizelou, with the main streets just behind it. From the *plateia*, as you face the sea, a long beach runs away to the right, backed by a scatter of tourist development and a valley with plastic greenhouses. To your left, running straight up northwards, is the harbour front, enclosed at the far end by a quay where the ferry docks. Steep and attractive streets, some with

The frescos of the Panagía Kera are one of the glories of Crete

EASTERN CRETE

Siteía, with its harbour backed by bright houses, is busier each year

broad steps, climb up the hill behind among freshly painted houses. This part of town appears light and airy; upper storeys enjoy excellent views. The Venetians fortified Siteía but it never came to much (the Venetian fortress has now been restored). The town's greatest son was the epic poet Vincenzos Kornaros. The Turks destroyed Siteía and let it lie for two centuries. Then from 1870, it began to come to life again, achieving the extremely pleasant atmosphere that distinguishes it today. There has been an **Archaeological Museum** here since 1984 and there is a **Folklore Museum**, run by volunteers and not always open when expected. The area is rich in grapes, generally on their way to becoming sultanas, and there is a lively sultana festival in mid-August.

SPINALÓGKA ISLAND

north of Ágios Nikólaos

The remarkable island of Spinalógka may be reached on caique trips direct from Ágios Nikólaos. The cruise, which is fairly lengthy, may also include a picnic and stops for swimming. Other trips, using smaller, local boats, run from the attractive village of Eloúnta (see **Accommodation**, page 82). The main feature of Spinalógka is its massive Venetian fortress. Like the island-fortress at the mouth of Soúda Bay, Spinalógka was virtually impregnable and held out against the Turks long after Crete had fallen. It was eventually handed over in 1715. From 1903 to 1957 it was a leper colony, said to have been the last in Europe. This gives an uneasy fascination to any tour.

ZÁKROS

25 miles (40km) southeast of Siteía

Zákros is a long way from anywhere and those who are only marginally interested in the Minoans may well be disappointed. But for some *aficionados*, this is the most inspirational of Minoan sites. The road to Káto (Lower) Zákros, the site of the palace, descends from Ano (Upper) Zákros, crossing slopes of a strange purplish hue. There is also a fine walk down through the ravine, though you will need precise instructions and should not venture here in bad or unsettled weather, as it is prone to flash floods. The ruins themselves lie close behind the sea, which has risen since Minoan days. Parts of the site are often semi-submerged.

The sense of distance and apartness conveyed by Zákros is largely an illusion. The palace was poised for trade with Egypt and the Middle East and Zákros must have been an important staging post. The very high quality of the artefacts found here (see gallery VIII in the Irakleío museum) indicates wealth and culture, at least in the palace community; the number and size of other Minoan sites in eastern Crete show that Zákros was by no means as isolated as it appears today. It had been thoroughly forgotten, however, even in Homeric legend, and was only rediscovered during the 1960s in a celebrated dig by Professor Nicolas Platon. Treasure after treasure was recovered from a palace which seems never to have been plundered and which is relatively easy for the visitor to understand today since the only ruins visible are those of the New Palace period.

A good beginning is to walk up to the higher part of the ruined Minoan town just behind the main palace; this provides an overview of the palace itself. It will quickly be apparent that it is laid out much like Knossos, Phaistos or Mália. There is a central courtyard, with sacred and cult chambers immediately to the west. Entry is by a gate in the northeast corner. Passing down a ramped passageway and turning right, the visitor will find a room which may have been used for ritual ablutions by those entering the palace. In front now, on the east side of the court, are what may have been the royal chambers, one of them constructed round a large cistern used for storage of water from an adjacent spring. Seawater and peasant plough have demolished the bulk of the ruins on this side.

Crossing the central court, the visitor will find on the west side the remains of a large hall and a light-well where the Zákros bull's head *rhyton* was found. Just near here, facing in a southwest direction, the visitor will see the ruined vestiges of a lustral basin and an archive room.

A treasury near the large hall remains contained the famous Zákros conical *rhyton* in rock crystal, smashed into hundreds of fragments and reassembled with infinite patience.

Closed: Monday.

Accommodation

The road to Eloúnta strikes northwest along the Ágios Nikólaos front, with interesting views of offshore islands. Immediately on the edge of Ágios Nikólaos, on the right, there is a famous hotel, the **Minos Beach** (tel: 0841 22345). This was the first in Crete to use the central block and outlying bungalow concept and the hotel became the smartest place on the island. Today, though it has been displaced from this role, it still has the feel of a substantial and well-heeled country hotel. Just a little further on, again to the right, comes the **Minos Palace Hotel** (tel: 0841 23801). A very swagger affair owned by the same company. Near by is a small Byzantine chapel with fragmentary decoration from the period of the Iconoclasts, when images of the human form were banned. The road soon climbs, offering fine views across the Gulf of Mirabello. Then it plunges down, reaching a turn to the **Eloúnta Beach Hotel** (tel: 0841 41412), successor to the Minos Beach as the smartest spot on Crete. This is built in block-and-bungalow style, very luxurious, but also making good use of ideas from

Cretan vernacular architecture. Other good hotels have now coalesced around this nucleus. A little further on is the **Astir Palace** (tel: 0841 41502), also an agreeable luxury class hotel. This is the most fashionable corner of Crete, and the village of Eloúnta, now very busy with visitors, follows shortly. The harbour lies along one side of the large village square. Well to the south of Ágios Nikólaos, some 9 miles (14km) round the gulf, lies the secluded and very pleasing deluxe

Where the smart set once stayed: the famous Minos Beach hotel

category **Istron Bay Hotel** (tel: 0841 61347). Protected by rocky capes to either side, the only buildings visible from the hotel are those of Ágios Nikólaos far across the water. There is a very friendly atmosphere, with good swimming in sea and pool, and tennis courts. Back in Ágios Nikólaos itself there are plenty of rooms to rent and the C-class **Calypso Hotel** (tel: 0841 41367) on the front would make a pleasant place to stay.

At Siteía there are the usual run of hotels – Nikos Andonidakis's **Ítanos Hotel** (tel: 0843 22146) is very standard at the corner of the Siteía 'L'; by pressing north along the front and one street back, you come at last to the modest but acceptable **Hotel Castello** (tel: 0843 23763). And if you enjoy extreme simplicity in a communal and floral atmosphere, then George and Katina Nikolorakis's **Seaside Pension** (tel: 0843 22815 or 22031), just behind the beach 200 yards (200m) past the bridge, may be the place for you – surely the friendliest spot in Crete.

Restaurants
In Siteía, the harbour front is the most animated part of town, with **Zorba's Taverna** considerably the largest restaurant. **To Steki**, by the bus station, however, seems totally genuine – pots of beans and hearty dishes seldom found in tourist venues. For nightlife, **Zorba's**, fast moving towards monopoly, maintains another popular establishment. (Shoppers should look in on **Sitian Arts** on V Kornarou, one street behind the front, for prettily decorated stones and local watercolours).

PEACE AND QUIET

Wildlife and Countryside in Crete
by Paul Sterry

Southernmost of the Aegean Islands, Crete is by far the largest, and has the most varied scenery, with idyllic coasts, freshwater marshes and the extensive and herb-rich *phrygana*, the latter being the open and grazed habitat so characteristic of most Greek islands.

Most unexpected of all, however, are the mountains, some of which rise to nearly 8,200 feet (2,500m) above sea level and remain snow covered long after the arrival of spring.

Gulls on Crete

Various species of gulls are sometimes seen feeding along the strand line in search of carrion, but many individuals have learnt that the fish remains discarded at the ports and harbours provide a much better living.

The yellow-legged gull is a frequent visitor to the coasts. Superficially resembling the herring gulls of northern Europe, these birds have striking yellow legs rather than pink legs seen in herring gulls. If you search among their numbers, particularly during spring and autumn, you may find an Audouin's gull, distinguishable by its smaller size and reddish legs and bill, or a slender-billed gull with its piercing pale eyes. Check Irakleío and Ágios Nikólaos harbours for gulls.

The limestone which comprises many of the peaks has encouraged a rich variety of flowering plants, and gorges, carved through the ranges, harbour rare birds and mammals among the stunning scenery of cypress, pine and wild fig trees. Crete's position midway between Greece, Turkey and North Africa, makes it an ideal place to witness migration during the spring and autumn, with many of the birds staying to breed. These supplement the numbers of year-round resident species, and compared to many other Greek islands, Crete's birdlife is surprisingly varied; almost every niche from mountain top to rocky coastal cliff has something to offer the birdwatcher.

Coasts and Seas

Dotted around the coastline, which comprises both sandy beaches and dramatic and inspiring cliffs, are quiet fishing villages and tranquil harbours. Visit any of these and the fishermen's catches and taverna menus will bear witness to the wealth of marine life that flourishes beneath the surface of the Mediterranean.

Do not expect to see much evidence of marine life on the seashore, however, because being effectively land-locked, the Mediterranean has a very small tidal range. Consequently, there are no rock-pools or mudflats to be exposed at low tide and birdlife on the seashore itself is rather limited.

Almost any beach or cove along the north coast can have migrant waders and little egrets if it is not too disturbed. The coast of Spinalógka Island is also good. The months of March, April and May are best for birdwatching, with migrant breeding species arriving from Africa to supplement the numbers of resident species. Migrants on their way further north in Europe also frequently stop off around the coast to rest and recuperate. Coastal cliffs may harbour both Sardinian warblers and Ruppell's warblers, the latter looking extremely attractive with their beady red eyes and black heads with bold, white moustachial stripes. Cirl buntings and sometimes even Cretzschmar's buntings may be lurking higher up the cliffs, while overhead, Eleonora's falcons, resident from May until September, dash through the air, catching migrant birds in flight.

Yellow-legged gulls are common around Crete's ports

Mountains, Cliffs and Gorges
Venture inland and the land soon rises up towards hills and mountains of dramatic proportions. This rugged side to the island's landscape is often overlooked by those tourists who linger on the beaches but it richly repays a visit: the scenery is dramatic and inspiring, with many of the summits rising to 6,500 feet (2,000m) or more above sea level, and the plants and animals to be seen in the remote regions are fascinating and varied.

The presence of mountains has been an important factor contributing to the diversity of the island's flora. While the plants of lowland Crete are often typical of other Greek islands, of those that grow on the mountains, a significant number occur nowhere else in the world.

PEACE AND QUIET

Many of the mountains' birds would also be out of place on most other Aegean islands, and the sight of eagles and vultures adds to the sense of isolation. Many of the peaks are composed of limestone, a rock which is vulnerable to erosion by the slight acidity of rainwater, and over the ages, rivers and torrents have carved spectacular gorges into many of Crete's mountains. Most famous of all is the Samaria Gorge, but others can be equally rewarding for the naturalist, their sides, like those of many of the steep mountains, being covered in shade- and moisture-loving plants. Higher up the mountain slopes, many of the plants acquire the same rounded and spiny 'hedgehog' appearance found in the *garigue* of the Balearic Islands. Here and there, however, beautiful patches of *Chiondoxa cretica* flower freely where the snow has recently melted, along with the crocus, *Crocus sieberi*. Birds such as the beautifully marked alpine accentor feed quietly among the vegetation, while overhead, choughs wheel noisily through the air, their splayed wing-tips resembling fingers. Inaccessible crags and fissures provide secure nesting sites for golden and Bonelli's eagles, large birds of prey which can be seen

Spring-flowering Crocus sieberi, a beautiful flower of the upper slopes

soaring high in the skies on outstretched wings. The road from Ágios Nikólaos to Lasíthiou passes through good mountain areas as it winds up through the hills. The Selinari Gorge, on the main road west from Ágios Nikólaos, has vultures, as does the road near Selia.

The White Mountains

Dominating western Crete, the White Mountains, or Lefká Óri, hold what is arguably the most impressive scenery on the island. Their peaks are among the highest, several exceeding 7,850 feet (2,400m) above sea level, and the white limestone rocks, from which they earned their name, encourage an incredible diversity of flowering plants. Immense gorges, such as Samaria, dissect these mountains, their inaccessible ledges providing nesting sites for eagles and vultures.

Mountain Forests

Out of reach of man and his grazing animals, some of the more remote and inaccessible slopes are covered with relict patches of forest comprising funeral cypress, *Cupressus sempervirens*. Among these trees, which are supposed to resemble a funereal flame, grow holm oaks and Kermes oaks that harbour woodland birds such as short-toed treecreeper, chaffinch and great tit.
In common with many other parts of the Mediterranean, centuries of clearance by man have denuded many slopes of their forest cover. It is usually only inaccessible areas that retain their trees.

Crossing the Plain of Omalós to the start of the Samaria Gorge, the visitor comes upon staggering views of the mountains, often snow-clad until late summer. Because of the altitude, many of the plants found here flower later in the year than those of the lowland coastal regions. From May until July a profusion of flowers appears, many endemic to Crete, some being unknown outside the White Mountains. The birdlife of the White Mountains is also rich and varied. Lower slopes support parties of chukars, close relatives of the red-legged partridge, and blue rock thrushes, while warblers lurk in the cover of low bushes. Overhead, birds of prey such as peregrine, Bonelli's eagle, golden eagle and griffon vulture soar on the thermals, sometimes being joined by lammergeiers. In the air these rare and majestic birds are recognised by their immense wingspan and wedge-shaped tail.

The lower slopes of the White Mountains are still forested, giving a glimpse of Crete as it once was

Like other vultures, they feed primarily on carrion, but have the remarkable habit of dropping bones, too large to break or digest whole, from a great height on to rocks, causing them to shatter.

The Samaria Gorge

Few visitors to the Samaria Gorge (Farángi Samariás) can fail to be impressed by its awesome scale. Carved over the millennia by rushing winter torrents, the gorge descends from the Plain of Omalós towards the sea and is home to a wealth of plant and animal life.

Although it is possible to walk the entire length of the gorge from May onwards, this lengthy journey should ideally only be undertaken by those who are fit and who are properly equipped for a long, and at times, very rough hike. The terrain is tough-going and flash-floods are not unknown and have caused fatalities even in recent years. However, a short excursion into the gorge is thoroughly worthwhile and will yield many of Samaria's botanical treasures while posing no safety risk.

Since the shade and humidity of the gorge's walls encourage a lengthy flowering period, there are interesting plants to be seen throughout the spring and summer. Many of the species are specially adapted to these damp conditions, thriving particularly well where water trickles over the rocks. Bellflowers, pinks and specialities such as *Symphyandra cretica* and Cretan ebony sometimes cascade down the rockfaces, safely out of reach of nibbling sheep and goats.

The steep sides of the Samaria Gorge (above) have a rich variety of flowers including the Cretan ebony (below)

Within the gorge itself, pines harbour migrant birds such as orphean warbler and redstart as well as resident short-toed treecreepers, the only species of treecreeper to be seen on the island. The shade which the trees cast on the woodland floor provides ideal conditions for the endemic Cretan cyclamen, while in more open areas, a variety of spring-flowering orchids grow among cistus bushes and the beautiful paeony, *Paeonia clusii.* As the gorge descends towards the sea, small parties of crag martins can be seen flying to and fro in front of the rockfaces. Alpine swifts dash through the air, and while you follow a party of these aerobatic birds with binoculars, griffon vultures may glide into the field of view.

Phrygana

Centuries of occupation by man have had a marked effect upon the vegetation of Crete. As with many other area around the Mediterranean, much of the evergreen woodland which once cloaked the region has long since been felled, leaving only relict patches of natural forest in a few gorges and on inaccessible mountain slopes. Man's domestic animals have also taken a toll on the landscape so that the colourful and shrubby *maquis* habitat, so typical of the French Riviera, is not widespread either and the resulting landscape, known as *phrygana*, is open and stony with only the occasional isolated tree to break the monotony.
Crete's climate has also influenced the vegetation of the *phrygana*: shade-loving plants cannot survive the hot, dry summers on the baking soils and even those species adapted to the harsh conditions generally wither by June. The winter rains induce new growth, however, and by the spring, the plants have burst into leaf and flower. To protect themselves from desiccation and to deter grazing animals, many of the *phrygana's* plants have developed natural defences. Some produce leaves which are wax-coated to reduce water loss, and spiny species of mullein grow with hairy-leaved sages. Among these, showy species such as fritillaries, birthworts and tassel hyacinths appear, mostly to die back soon after flowering. Some of the *phrygana* plants are endemic to Crete, and especially attractive is the Cretan ebony, *Ebenus*

PEACE AND QUIET

cretica, large clumps of which produce beautiful heads of pink flowers in spring.

Skinks and lizards hunt insects on the dry *phrygana* soil and chukars are sometimes heard calling. Where the vegetation is dense enough, various warblers may be found. Hillsides often have blue rock thrushes, males of which sometimes sing from rocky outcrops.

Buntings

Two potentially confusing species of bunting are found on Crete, namely Ortolan and Cretzschmar's buntings. These birds often feed on the ground and can be quite confiding. Females are always difficult to distinguish, but a good look at the colours of males should separate them. Although both have brick-red plumages, ortolans have a dull green head with a yellow throat, while Cretzschmar's have a blue head with red throat.

Phrygana habitat abounds in lowland Crete; good areas can also be found on Spinalógka Island. Also check around the Phaistos Minoan Palace and the Préveli Monastery.

Spring Flowers

Come to Crete in the height of summer and the landscape of the uncultivated lowlands will be almost universally brown and lifeless. The soil is parched and the unremitting heat and lack of water will have shrivelled all but the hardiest of shrubs and evergreen trees. However, visit the island again in spring and things will be altogether different:

Phrygana *habitat is rich in birds and spring flowers*

the leaves are green and flowers in a multitude of colours greet the eye. To understand this almost miraculous transformation you need to appreciate the nature of the Mediterranean climate, which shows striking seasonal variation. Winters are generally mild and wet but from late spring until autumn, sunshine is virtually guaranteed and rain is almost unknown. Plants take advantage of this predictable cycle, growing and producing their leaves in the winter and lying dormant during the summer. Many species flower in the spring, at the end of the growing season and before the onset of the summer drought, and shortly afterwards they wither away above ground, reappearing only after the first autumn rains. To escape the arid summers, plants have developed a number of strategies: underground tubers, bulbs and rhizomes are common and many species are annual, that is they live only one season, germinating in the autumn.

However, what is true for lowland Crete is not necessarily true for the mountains, since altitude has a profoundly modifying effect on the climate. With over 1,500 species of plants to be found in Crete, there is no shortage of flowers to be seen in the spring and from March to June, tulips, poppies and flaxes adorn the fields. Some species, such as the crown anemone, *Anemone coronaria*, tassel hyacinth and many of the orchids, are widespread in the eastern

Mediterranean, while others have a more restricted distribution. Because of Crete's isolation as an island and its variety of habitats, around 100 species are endemic, that is they are found nowhere else in the world. There are endemic species of friar's cowl, birthwort, tulip and pink, but one of the most attractive is the cyclamen, *Cyclamen creticum*. Preferring to grow under the shade of trees, the leaves sometimes form little carpets and the delicate white flowers appear in March and April.

Plains and Agricultural Land

In contrast to the barren and stony hillsides with poor soils, many of the lowland valleys and plains are comparatively fertile and where an adequate water supply persists throughout the summer, a wide range of crops is grown. That most characteristic tree of the Mediterranean, the olive, is as widespread today as it has been for centuries and lemons, carobs, figs, almonds and even corn are also commonly grown. The cultivated fields provide feeding grounds for larks and pipits, while the leafy shade of orchards and olive groves is ideal for shrikes and warblers. Warmth and sunshine are not in short supply but water, however, is a decidedly scarce commodity. Men go to great lengths to ensure a permanent irrigation supply, and nowhere more so than on the Lasíthiou Plateau in eastern Crete. Surrounded by mountains, the area is famous for the water-pumping windmills which dot the mosaic of fields and keep them green and lush all year round. By day, geckos and wall lizards scurry among the ground

Cretan water-pumping windmills irrigate the Lasíthiou Plain

Green toads are strictly nocturnal

vegetation, while chameleons are occasionally seen sitting motionless and camouflaged in the branches of shrubs and trees. After dark, balkan whip snakes and cat snakes venture out of cover in search of a meal, and boldly marked green toads patrol for insects.

Recently tilled fields are the haunt of skylarks, short-toed larks and exotic looking hoopoes that probe the soil with their long beaks. Although their black and white barred wings make them conspicuous in flight, they can be extremely inconspicuous on the ground as they shuffle along the furrows. Tawny pipits, wheatears and black-eared wheatears also prefer these open fields where insects are easy to find, and, in spring, males of the latter species are especially resplendent with their black, white and fawn plumage. Overhead wires and dead branches provide ideal perches for colourful bee-eaters who launch themselves into the air after insect prey. Their liquid calls are a familiar sound in lowland Crete in spring. To reach the Lasíthiou Plain drive up the hairpin road which runs west from Ágios Nikólaos. Other areas of agricultural land can be found along the road which runs along the south coast of Crete.

Marshes and Saltpans

Around the coast of Crete, and especially between Irákleío and Siteía, several small areas of marshes and saltpans offer a habitat which contrasts markedly with the arid interior of the island. Wetlands, not only on Crete but throughout the eastern Mediterranean as a whole, are coming increasingly under threat from disturbance and tourist development. Hopefully, with a growing awareness of their importance both in terms of the island's ecology and as a lure to naturalist holidaymakers, the

PEACE AND QUIET

A migrant wood sandpiper

authorities may yet recognise their true value.

Marsh frogs and dice snakes are constant residents of the marshes but the species of birds vary throughout the year. From early spring until the summer, a variety of migrant waders, including greenshank, wood and marsh sandpipers, little ringed plovers and little stint might be seen. The length of their legs determines how deep they can wade in the water, but by contrast, the depth of water presents few problems for black-winged stilts. They have such long legs that they can wade almost anywhere and if they get out of their depth, they resort to swimming.

Little egrets, elegant with their pure white plumage and long plumes, sometimes feed among the smaller waders. Purple herons, however, prefer to stay in the cover provided by reedbeds and other aquatic vegetation, and little bitterns, which are equally secretive, are seldom seen except in flight. Great reed warblers are bolder, however, and often sing their loud, guttural song from the tops of the reeds.

The evaporating, briny waters of saltpans are too hostile an environment for most aquatic creatures to survive. However, brine shrimps and brine flies both thrive under these conditions and their numbers provide a feast for both stilts and

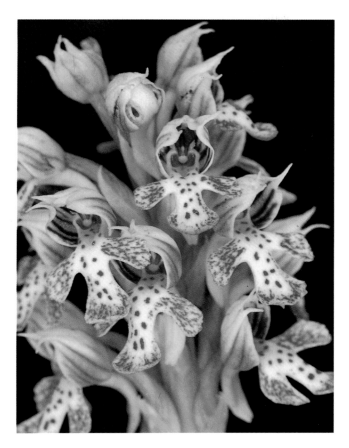

A colourful milky orchid

avocets, the latter being elegant, black and white birds with long up-turned bills with which they scythe the water in search of prey. As the water finally dries up, the surface of the cracked mud attracts short-toed larks, Kentish plovers and pratincoles. Wetland sites to visit include Lake Kournas and the Agía Reservoir near Ágios Nikólaos. There is a marsh near the coast 2 miles (3km) east of Mália and a lake at Georgeopolis. Development threatens many of these sites.

Orchids

Crete is justly famous for its spring flowers, and in particular for its native, wild orchids, several of which are endemic to the island. The list of orchids is

PEACE AND QUIET

long, 20 or more species often being recorded by visitors in a week in April, with the variation in their appearance almost endless. Some of the species occur in a variety of forms and many lovers of wild orchids pay regular spring homage to Crete to delight in nothing but its wealth of orchids.

> ### Orchid Biology
> Part of the fascinating lure of orchids comes from their appearance, the flowers often being a beautiful shape and colour. Some are fragrant and thereby attract pollinating insects, but many others do so by mimicking insect members of the opposite sex. In the bee orchid family, in particular, this is most highly developed, the furry lower lips of the flowers often looking extremely life-like.
> The life history of orchids is also intriguing since in most cases, seeds will not germinate successfully if a partnership with a special fungal mycelium has not developed. Orchids are generally slow-growing, with sometimes as much as five years elapsing between germination and the appearance of leaves and flowers above ground.

On the open *phrygana* habitat, characterised by stony ground with scattered clumps of low vegetation, half a dozen or more species or forms of the genus *Ophrys* (bee orchids) can be found, including the endemic Cretan ophrys. Spikes of violet limodore prefer to grow where there is shade and are sometimes found in the company of dense-flowered orchids, whose thin, compact spikes of

Spitzel's orchid

small white flowers can be difficult to spot.

The genus *Orchis* is also well represented on Crete by plants with often bizarre names like monkey orchid, naked man orchid and bug orchid. Grassy patches often support the beautiful milky orchid, whose flowers resemble little dolls in brightly coloured dresses, while at higher altitudes, Spitzel's orchids produce flower spikes of a rich purple colour. The giant orchid, which more than lives up to its name, also grows on Crete, but since it flowers early in the year it has often withered to a brown spike before most visitors arrive.

Spring Migration

Lying less than 250 miles (400km) from the coast of North Africa, Crete is an ideal 'stepping-stone' for migrant birds heading north across the Mediterranean after a winter south of the equator. From March until May, thousands of birds pass through the island and, depending upon the prevailing weather conditions, many stop off to feed and replenish their reserves. Some of the migrants fly no further than Crete itself and, compared to most other Greek islands, its list of breeding species is rich, but many others continue the journey to northern Europe. Among the first to arrive are yellow wagtails, long-tailed birds which haunt fields and marshes on migration. At first, the observer may be confused into thinking that several species are present, but in fact yellow wagtails occur in a variety of colour forms or races, each one breeding in a different part of Europe. To distinguish them, you must study the head pattern carefully, but since these charming little birds are extremely active this is often easier said than done.

Even on migration, birds are attracted to the habitat to which they are normally accustomed and so, not surprisingly, marshes attract waders, terns and ducks. Garganey, drakes of which have elegantly marked head patterns, dabble among the vegetation, taking to the wing at the slightest danger, when the blue wing-panels and characteristic 'rattling' call help with their identification. Waders such as wood sandpipers, on the other hand, are often more confiding, allowing excellent views of their smart, spangled plumage. Around the coasts, olive groves and even small patches of vegetation may harbour warblers and chats in spring, the best time of day for searching being just after dawn. Since passerine birds generally migrate by night and make for cover at the first sign of light, coastal bushes are often the

Garganey haunt Crete's marshes in March and April

PEACE AND QUIET

first opportunity they have to rest. If they are not disturbed, they will stay here for several hours before they gradually drift off northwards, and shrikes, subalpine, Bonelli's and willow warblers, and pied and collared flycatchers are all regularly seen. Later in the day, things become quiet as the migrants disperse, but there is always a chance of seeing a party of bee-eaters flying in off the sea. Ideal weather conditions are not necessarily good for birdwatchers. During clear, calm conditions the migrants are likely to continue their journey northwards in spring. If, however, cloudy conditions or rain sets in during the night then the birds may become ground, especially in areas around the coast.

Found nowhere else in Greece, the chameleon is a common resident of scrub in lowland Crete

Chameleons

Islands normally have comparatively fewer species of animals than adjacent areas of mainland, this being particularly true of terrestrial creatures, such as reptiles, which cannot fly. However, partly because of its size and partly due to the geological history of the Mediterranean, Crete has 12 resident species of snakes and lizards, including one, the chameleon, not found anywhere else in Greece. Chameleons prefer bushes and trees even where their superbly camouflaged bodies can be difficult to spot. This camouflage not only serves to protect them from enemies, however, but also to render them inconspicuous to their insect prey. By contrast with its slow-motion movement, the action of the Chameleon's tongue is like lightning and the prey is caught in the blink of an eye.

SHOPPING

Crete produces some handsome
and individual craft items and
any number of tourist souvenirs.
But in general shopping does not
figure outstandingly among
holiday activities. There is too
much else to do and too little in
Crete that is really exceptional.
Weaving is the most visible and
colourful of Cretan crafts. It is
practised particularly in the
mountain villages of Kritsá and
Anógia. Colours are often very
striking; materials range from
relatively suave to awesomely
prickly. The best buys may be
bedspreads, rugs or sturdy
shopping bags. Greek shoulder
bags are also attractive. In Crete
there is a special variety used by
shepherds, with a draw-string to
pull the bag tight and woollen
cords to go over both shoulders
like a small knapsack. Highly
recommended. Old woven items
are also available in some
specialist shops – very beautiful
and very expensive.
Lace is still made in Crete but
many of the old stitches appear
to have been lost or have
become unprofitable. Antique
lace, when available, can be
beautiful, though pricey. Boots
are still hand-made in Crete and
can be very fine (see
Réthymno). There are locally-
made, wooden-handled clasp-
knives, too, with violent-looking
serrated blades and other
equally earthy products from an
island still predominantly
agricultural.
Jewellery has long been made in
Crete and here standards are
looking up remarkably. Where
once the main offering consisted

Handmade craft items for sale

almost entirely of crude replicas
of Minoan jewellery, there are
now individual modern items,
often in gold, alongside quite
high quality replicas. This
coincides with the arrival of
fashion boutiques in places like
Irakleio and Hersonisos.

FOOD AND DRINK

Food

For true Greek food it is
necessary to look to the host of
informal tavernas, often by
beaches and in seaside villages,
with umbrellas or bamboo
awnings and outdoor tables
closely crowded together; to the
estiatoria, fairly modest
restaurants found mostly in
towns, where a wider variety of
dishes is likely to be served; to
the *psistaria*, where lamb and
other meats are roasted on the
spit, wafting delicious smells into
the neighbouring air; and, lastly,
to the few rather more formal
restaurants in smarter parts of
towns.

FOOD AND DRINK

In all these it is possible to eat interestingly – though people do tend to complain of the quantity of olive oil. Others resent the fact that everything is served lukewarm – which is how the Greeks and many other people in hot countries like it. But these barriers drop away as one gets into the spirit of the island. The only real problem is that in the smaller places, down towards the end of the supply line, variety may diminish dramatically in high season. Greek starters (*mezedes*) are now well-known outside Greece and have even reached Crete which used not to go in for them.

Taramosalata, smoked cod's roe purée, is of variable quality; *tzatsiki* is yogurt and cucumber, generally with lots of garlic. *Melitzanosalata*, literally aubergine salad, is often the most tasty of the dips.

Meat dishes are generally simple. *Souvlaki*, chunks of meat on a skewer, is sold in restaurants and also as a fast food. Lamb chops with a few chips, or French fries (*paidakia*) are a common stand-by. So is chicken (*kotopoulo*) and of course eggs (one egg, *avga*; two eggs, *avgata*). Omelette is *omeleta*. Restaurants and tavernas may serve various kind of stew, among them *stifado* – beef with tomato and onion. There are also a number of baked dishes. Best known is moussaka – mince, aubergine and bechamel. Spit-roast meat is sold by the kilo, which makes it look more expensive on menus that it turns out to be.

Fish is good but expensive and often, likewise, sold by the kilo. Pick your own where possible, either in the kitchen or from the fridge. Red mullet (*barbounia*) are much revered. Swordfish (*ksifias*) and octopus (*ktapodi*) are good, and squid (*kalamari*) is excellent but can be expensive.

In Cretan restaurants, choose from a selection of traditional dishes

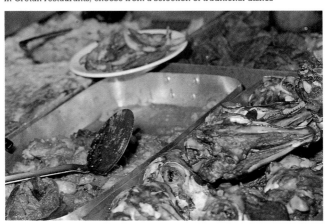

Vegetables are often very good; tomatoes are the summer staple. *Horiatiki* or 'village' salads consist of tomatoes, oil, onions, olives and anything else going, with a cube of fresh goat's cheese called *feta* resting on top. This makes a refreshing accompaniment to any meal. There are also good stewed vegetables. *Fasoulada*, green beans stewed in tomatoes, can be excellent.

Greeks are not generally big dessert eaters, but delicious, honey-rich pastries are widely sold. Find your local patisserie (*zacharoplasteion*) and all too probably you will be tempted by *baklava* (pastry, honey and nuts)

Local wines can be excellent

Greek Coffee

Greek coffee is the same as Turkish, the water boiled up with the grounds in tiny individual pots and served in tiny cups. The coffee is thick and usually sweet. *Metrio* – or medium – is the normal degree of sweetness. *Sketo* means 'no sugar', *glyko* very sweet.

Tavernas seldom serve coffee, and some establishments serve only Nescafé.

In the days before tourism, the proper place for a Greek man to take coffee was the *kafeneion*, often a small and dusty little room with upright, wicker-bottomed chairs and old men reading newspapers.

Women were not particularly welcome. Some traditional *kafeneia* still survive, even in tourist areas, but foreign women are now treated as honorary men. There are also cafeterias of a more obviously European type.

or the equally fattening and delicious *kataifi* (this looks like shredded wheat, also filled with honey and nuts).

Drink

Crete is a wine-producing and wine-drinking island. There are no amazingly high quality wines but some of the labelled Cretan brands are increasingly good and 'loose' village wines, sold by the kilo in restaurants (*ena kilo* is one kilo, *miso* is half, about the same as a litre or half-litre bottle) can be satisfactorily soothing. Bottled wines from elsewhere in Greece are also available. There is red (*mavro*, meaning, literally, black), white (*aspro*), rosé (*kokkino*, literally red) and resin-tasting *retsina*, originally made in Attica but now produced in Crete too. Light Continental beer is locally produced and widely drunk, and foreign beers are now also brewed under licence.

ACCOMMODATION

The best known Greek aperitif is *ouzo*, a colourless, aniseed-flavoured drink which turns white when water is added. Cretans drink home-made *tsikoudia*, also known as *raki*. This is a grape-based distilled liquor, equivalent to French marc or Italian grappa, very strong and for some tastes much preferable to ouzo. Aperitifs are served with some small morsel of food called *meze*, or *mezedes* in the plural. This can extend to specially-ordered snacks, grilled octopus or sardines, shellfish, etc – often delicious though potentially expensive.

ACCOMMODATION

The key to understanding accommodation in Crete, and to much else besides, is the realisation that two systems of tourism and two distinct tourist economies flourish side by side. One is the world of the pre-booked package holiday, and the other belongs to the independent traveller. Both groups are on the whole well served.

The great volume of package holidays are taken in hotels. There are six grades of hotel: luxury (L), and then from A to E. Category C hotels are moderate, but by the time D and E are reached, hotels are extremely simple, though usually clean and perfectly decent. Most of the big package hotels are strung out along the north coast beaches, or located in the north coast resorts. They are sometimes out of scale against their settings but generally acceptable inside. Some are very good and have all kinds of facilities. But while they are fine for sun and sea, they may

The village of Eloúnta – in an area popular with visitors

isolate the visitor a little from Cretan life. Almost all these hotels are closed in winter. There is one particular style of hotel in Crete which has become quite characteristic of the island. In this type, there will normally be a central building for reception, dining room, other essential services and a limited number of bedrooms. Most of the bedrooms, however, are in bungalows or simple two-storey buildings, likewise described as bungalows, and almost always set among gardens. The first Cretan hotel on this pattern was the Minos Beach in Ágios Nikólaos. It was followed by the Astir Palace and Eloúnta Beach Hotels, both near the village of Eloúnta, a little north of Ágios Nikólaos. The Eloúnta Beach is regarded as Crete's leading

ACCOMMODATION

Inexpensive Independence

Some independent travellers will be sufficiently well-funded to stay in the better hotels. The package holiday hotels are not geared up to single-night stays and may prove over-expensive, but there are decent hotels in all the towns, ranging from A-class downwards. There is usually a cluster of acceptable B- and C-class hotels around bus stations. There is also a growing network of small hotels in interesting and unlikely places. The other great standby, mainly popular with backpackers and the young, is 'rent rooms'. There are numerous rooms to rent in every town and many villages and these are generally adequate, sometimes very pleasant. The hospitality and friendliness of owners can be a pleasure. But do see the room before taking it, agree a price and expect to pay extra for showers. People with rooms to rent will often approach you or you can enquire at the local Tourist Police Office, the Municipal Tourist Information Office or in any café or taverna. Bookings can also be made through local travel agents. There is also a limited number of pensions, youth hostels and campsites.

hotel, and very fine it is too. Many newer hotels, generally described in this guide as 'block-and-bungalow', have been built in imitation of Minos Beach and Eloúnta Beach. Others, though, are simple blocks of the kind often found in Spain.

'Villas', ranging from well-appointed houses to new and rather charmless little dwellings, are also pre-let to package holidaymakers. Tour companies arrange in advance to operate them for the whole of a season and the villa comes as part of a package including flight and possibly hire-car.

Advance reservation for all the above style of accommodation can be made through the Hellenic Chamber of Hotels, 24 Stadiou Street, 105 64 Athens (fax: 3225 449 or 3236 962). Independent travellers must naturally take things as they find them. In terms of accommodation, they may not find very much in July and August. Crete's high-season popularity has at the moment somewhat outstripped provision. But in winter, spring and autumn this is a marvellous way to visit Crete. The rugged landscape means that mass tourism has by no means reached every corner; the sense of discovery endures, and out of season, even in remote places, there is almost somewhere reasonable to stay the night.

IRAKLEÍO

October–January

May–August

WEATHER AND WHEN TO GO

Crete, the most southerly of Greek islands, has a robust climate, fresh and delicious in spring, very hot in summer, warm and serene in autumn and generally mild in winter. Like almost all the Mediterranean, it can be very windy in summer. The *meltemi* blows hard out of the north for days at a time and there is a rarer and unpleasant wind which comes up from the Sahara laden with sand and dust. In winter, when it rains, it rains – then generally cheers up again. It can also be surprisingly cold in short bursts between November and February. The mountains are snow-covered from autumn to late spring. Summer clothing along the beaches should be very light. A jacket or jersey is only a marginal necessity and most people bring far more clothes than they actually use. In winter, it pays to pack on the opposite principle. Bring more warm clothes than you think you should. Those planning to walk or sleep at higher altitudes should reckon with cold nights in summer and be properly dressed and equipped in winter.

SPECIAL EVENTS

There are many festivals and festivities, mainly local. The principal events are listed below. The year's major festival is the Greek Orthodox Easter, falling up to a month later than the Catholic/Protestant Easter. See also **Holidays** in the **Directory** section.

May
Chaniá Battle of Crete remembered in the last week in May in a series of events, including Cretan dancing in the Public Gardens.

July
Réthymno Wine Festival in the town park for a week in late July.

August
Assumption of the Virgin, 15 August.
Irakleío Feast of St Titus, patron saint of Crete, 25 August.

Visitors can enjoy folk music and dancing at a 'Cretan evening'

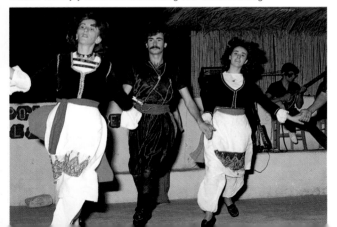

CULTURE, ENTERTAINMENT AND NIGHTLIFE

Most hotels have their own discos and all the resorts offer a modicum of choice. Greek and specifically Cretan music can provide a unique experience. The *bouzouki* is a kind of mandolin; much Greek popular music is written for it. Bouzouki places are usually out of town, expensive, and start late, and among the few spots where you are likely to see Greeks drink at all heavily. The three-stringed lyre or *lyra* is the real Cretan instrument, powerful and plangent.

Crete has culture in abundance in its ancient and medieval art and architecture. The contemporary contribution is smaller. There are sometimes exhibitions of paintings in the church of Ágios Títos in Irakleío and various theatrical events. There are two great popular entertainments. The first is the cinema. Films are usually shown in their language of origin, with subtitles. Many towns have outdoor cinemas in summer – operating after dark, of course. The other entertainment, in the bigger towns, is the *volta*, an evening stroll along one or two mutually agreed streets in which the whole populace participates.

HOW TO BE A LOCAL

- Return the straightforward friendliness offered by Cretans – this happens even in crowded resorts, and it is churlish not to respond.
- Women may have special problems – besides the

In conservative Crete, the café is still largely a male domain

traditional friendliness, there are now plenty of young men eager for involvement (to put it politely) with foreigners, and this may require an active response. *Ochi* means 'no';

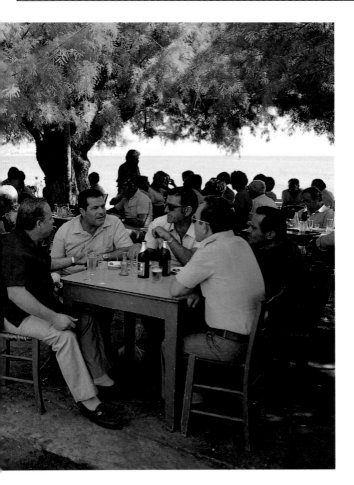

figete means 'go away'; *neh*, surprisingly, means 'yes'.

● If you are offered hospitality in the villages, be assured that it is offered in genuine sincerity, and with the real hope that you will accept. This reflects a tradition unbroken since the age of Homer, and is only gradually coming under threat. Sometimes you can be pressed to stay when you really want to go, and it can be difficult to beat a courteous retreat.

● In villages women will feel more comfortable if they dress modestly. In churches and monasteries, respectful dress is positively required, often by written signs – evidence that tourist behaviour has not always been up to the mark. Crete is still a very conservative society.

● Although topless swimming and nude bathing are now quite common, it is unwelcome to Cretans except where custom sanctions it. It is not good manners for people of either sex to strip off on a beach close to a country village.

CHILDREN

Children can have a wonderful time in Crete, provided they are given a day or two for adjustment and protected from the sun for a little longer at the start than may seem reasonable to them. The sea on its own is enough to ensure happiness at first; and for teenagers there are watersports – water-skiing or windsurfing – in many of the resorts. So far as interference or molestation is concerned, Greece is child-loving. Children are part of things in a

way they are not in northern Europe – welcome in restaurants, bars and tavernas.

TIGHT BUDGET

● Small pensions and 'rent rooms' provide very cheap accommodation for the independent traveller.
● For lower rates be prepared to stay in the outskirts of towns and a fair hike from the beach.
● Use buses for transport. The network is better each year.
● Eat like a local. Cheese, bread and vegetables are fresh, nutritious and cheap. Remember, Crete may be an island but fresh fish is often expensive. Eat in a taverna rather than a hotel restaurant. Wine may be cheaper than beer.
● Cretans may prove astonishingly hospitable; do not abuse this hospitality. Villagers will usually be poorer than you.

Vái beach: paradise for sun-lovers

DIRECTORY

Arriving

By Air The main international airport, serving the centre and east, is Irakleío, 3 miles (5km) from town. It has a snack bar, a restaurant and a duty free shop for departures. There is easy connection with town by bus or taxi. Chaniá airport, 7 miles (12km) from town and the point of arrival for western Crete, is considerably quieter. There is a smaller airport at Siteía in the east, internal only, but good for island hopping.

By Sea There are daily car and passenger ferry services from Piraeus, the port of Athens and the hub of island shipping. These go to Irakleío and Chaniá (Soúda Bay) taking 12 hours. The arrival at Soúda Bay with views of the White Mountains above, is the most dramatic way of reaching Crete. There are regular arrivals in Irakleío via Santorini (Thera), a fine volcanic island north of Crete. There is a service from Githion in the Peloponnese to Kastélli Kissámou in the west and sailings – which may vary from year to year – eastwards to Rhodes and the Dodecanese Islands from Ágios Nikólaos and Siteía. There is also a fast hydrofoil service between Irakleío and the Cyclades (Santorini, Ios, Paros, Naxos and Mykonos), and irregular connections between Crete and Italy.

Camping

In theory, camping is only permitted on official sites. Sleeping out on the beaches is still quite common, though, as one may observe in remoter spots like Soúgia in southwest Crete. There are a number of organised camping sites in both larger and smaller places.

Chemist see **Pharmacies**

Crime

The crime rate in Crete is very low. There is some suggestion that foreign visitors are not above a little petty thieving, so normal prudence, at least, will be required.

Foreigners are strongly advised not to import or use drugs in Greece. Penalties for possession are considerable; and long sentences await those caught dealing. Casual camping and nude bathing are both technically illegal.

Customs Regulations

Visitors from within the EU may bring in duty-free the following goods:
800 cigarettes or 400 cigarillos or 200 cigars or 1kg (2.2lbs) tobacco (18 years or over);
20 litres spirits or 10 litres wine or liqueurs (18 years or over);
75g perfume; 0.25 litre toilet water; and gifts.
There are slightly more generous allowances if tax and duty have been paid by passengers arriving from EU countries. For currency restrictions see **Money Matters**, page 116.

Domestic Travel

Air There are numerous flights each day between Athens and both Irakleío and Chaniá (for airports, see **Arriving**, page 109) taking 45 minutes. Irakleío

DIRECTORY

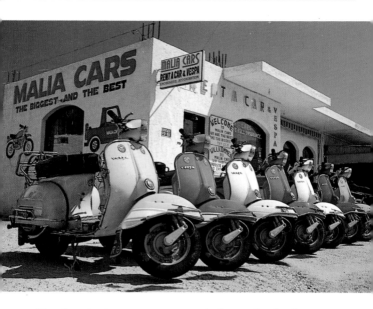

Mopeds can be hired in any resort

has flights to Rhodes and Thessaloniki. Siteía has flights to Karpathos and Kasos.

Bus The service along the north coast's New Road, from Chaniá to Ágios Nikólaos, is fast and regular. Irakleío has four bus stations serving different quarters of the compass and a change of bus may necessitate a change of bus station, too. There are good connections between the four 'nome' capitals and smaller towns in their areas. There is also an elaborate network of village buses, though these are likely to go into town in the morning and return in the afternoon, the wrong way round for many tourists. Tickets for longer journeys should be bought at the bus station, for shorter journeys on the bus.

Taxi These are reasonably priced and readily available. Two or three people travelling together may well find taxis handy for whole or half-day excursions, with reasonable fares – but do agree the price with the driver beforehand. Villages have special country taxis, marked *Agoraion* – in the Greek alphabet – and compensate for any gaps in the bus service.

Ferry There are numerous ferries from Piraeus and other Greek islands (see **Arriving**, page 109). Crete's own island dependencies, notably Gávdos off the southwest coast, can also be reached by sea.

Walking Crete offers some of the best walking in Europe, ranging from strolls through rich landscapes to arduous trails high among limestone crags. Walking in Crete is also a wonderful way to meet rural people. Some of the most used trails are waymarked with paint splodges, but people attempting the harder walks should be advised that experience really is required – as well as good boots. For advice, contact Greek Mountaineering Club (tel: 081 227609) or OYK (Long Distance Club of Crete – tel: 081 228225).

Driving

Breakdown
A warning triangle should be set out 110 yards (100m) behind the car, and flashing hazard lights turned on.

A donkey is the only transport to some places off the beaten track

Car hire firms recommend that their customers contact them in the event of breakdown, and they will make arrangements. The police, the National Tourist Organisation and managements of large hotels are also helpful. Other motorists and passers-by can be extraordinarily kind while mechanics are often more resourceful than in northern Europe.

ELPA, the Automobile and Touring Club of Greece, will help members of affiliated AIT clubs. Telephone numbers are: Ágios Nikólaos, 0841 22620; Irakleío, 081 289440; Chaniá, 0821 96611; Réthymno, 0831 54554; or call 104 (Emergency Road Assistance).

Car Rental
Car hire is now a major industry in Crete with the normal range of hire cars on offer, as well as

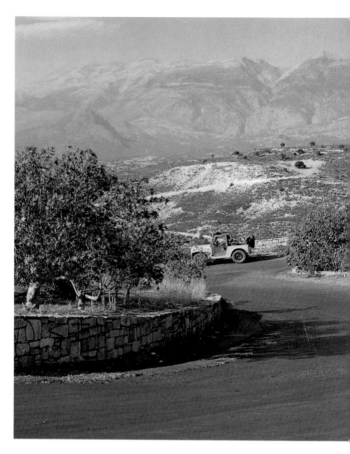

four-wheel-drive vehicles, often open-topped. International companies such as Hertz and Avis operate on the island; there are also numerous local companies. Many visitors arrange in advance to collect vehicles at the airport. Cars may be hired locally in resorts for a few days only or even a single day. Cars should always be looked over for standards of maintenance and cleaning before they are accepted. Credit card is the preferred method of payment; if by cash, a large deposit will be required. A driving licence in force for more than a year will be requested; otherwise an international driving permit. All resorts have motor-bikes and mopeds for hire.

On the road near Phaistos: the independent motorist can enjoy Crete's most spectacular scenery

Documents and Equipment

For car hire: A valid, full driving licence and, probably, passport will need to be shown, if not surrendered. Age policy varies but for most companies you must be 23 or over.

For driving own car: To have reached Greece, unless you have stayed in EU countries all the way, you will probably have needed an international driving licence and green insurance card (without which your cover will be third party only). Vehicle registration documents should also be carried. Check special requirements for countries *en route*.

For Greece, the vehicle should have a nationality plate or sticker; first aid kit; fire extinguisher; and a red warning triangle.

Entry Formalities

The government is anxious that foreigners should not sell their vehicles during a stay of less than 6 months. After this period, you are free to sell your vehicle. Contact the nearest Customs office for full details.

Fuel

Fuel is plentiful in towns but may be harder to find in rural areas; unleaded may also be difficult to find. If you are planning a longish trip in remote parts, it is best to start with a full tank. It is illegal to carry petrol in cans in vehicles.

Driving in Crete

This is certainly the easiest way to see the island but not as easy as all that. The New Road along the north coast is fast and modern, with some of it dual carriageway. Roads to other towns and all major historical and archaeological sites are asphalt and the number of dirt roads is dwindling annually, if a little fitfully, as modernisation progresses. Most of the dirt roads are now fine – but there are hazards. Potholes may be impressive, especially if there are road works anywhere near. Winter rain and landslips can mean that edges of otherwise well maintained roads disappear rather suddenly. Very minor roads still sometimes give up unexpectedly. And some of the gradients are steep, with little or no protection. Greek drivers expect you to blow your horn as you approach blind corners. They do not use their rear mirrors excessively and you are meant to hoot before overtaking. In summary, the experience is exhilarating but it is important to drive carefully and be ready for almost anything.

Insurance
Comprehensive cover is recommended both for own and hire cars. Insurance giving cover for injury, hospitalisation, and air-ambulance transport home is also desirable.

Road Signs
Road signs follow standard European conventions though there may be some additional signs in Greek only. Place names on signposts are usually given in the Latin as well as the Greek alphabet. Spelling normally follows the new phonetic version (*eg* Festos for the more customary Phaistos) and is not always immediately obvious.

Seat Belts
Seat belts must be worn in front and rear seats and children under 10 must sit in the rear. There are on-the-spot fines for failure to comply.

Speed Limits
50kph (31mph) in towns; 80kph (50 mph) on provincial roads; 100kph (62 mph) elsewhere – motorbikes 70kph (43 mph).

Electricity
Crete runs on 220 volts AC. Supplies in rural areas are unpredictable.

Embassies and Consulates
Embassies (all in Athens):
British: 1 Ploutarchou Street, 106–75 Athens (tel: 723 62 11).
US: Vas Sofias Avenue 91, 115–21 Athens (tel: 721 29 51, 721 84 00).

Canadian: 4 Gennadious Street, Ypsilantou, 115–21 Athens (tel: 723 95 11).
British Consulate (in Crete): 16 Papalexantrou Street, Irakleío (tel: 081 22 4012).

Emergency Telephone Numbers
General emergency: 100
First aid/ambulance: 166
Police: 171
Tourist Police: 104

Entertainment Information
Hotel desks are well informed about local events, as is the

National Tourist Organisation (NTOG or EOT, see **Tourist Offices**, page 121).

Entry Formalities see also **Domestic Travel/Driving**, page 112
Visitors from EU countries issuing identity cards require only these. Entry is for three months, generally renewable. Eastern bloc visitors require visas, and must register with the immigration authorities (Aliens Department) within 48 hours of arrival. Visitors from the US and Canada do not require visas.

Health
For visitors from Europe and North America, there are no special health regulations affecting Greece. But yellow fever vaccinations are required for those arriving within six days of leaving an infected area. Under EU agreements European visitors can receive free medical treatment. Form E111 must be obtained before leaving home. But it is always a sensible precaution to take out extra medical insurance in case of serious illness. Some package tours offer medical insurance at extra charge. Ensure that it covers motor accidents and the cost of an air-ambulance to take you to the mainland, or to fly you home if necessary.
Private doctors are expensive. You will have to pay them after receiving treatment and claim on your insurance when you return home. The Tourist Police can supply addresses and

Information on local events is available in many hotels

DIRECTORY

telephone numbers of local doctors and hospitals. For minor complaints, consult pharmacists (*farmakio*). (See **Pharmacies** page 118.)

Holidays, Public and Religious

New Year's Day: 1 January
Epiphany (exchange of Christmas presents): 6 January
Kathara Deftera ('Clean Monday'): celebration at entry to Lent, preceded by three weeks of lively carnival
Independence Day: 25 March
Labour Day: 1 May
Greek Orthodox Easter: Friday to Monday, falling up to a month later than Catholic/Protestant Easter
Ascension Day: date determined by Easter
Assumption of the Virgin: 15 August
Ochi or 'No' Day: 28 October (celebrates Greece's one word reply to Italian ultimatum, World War II)
Christmas Day: 25 December
St Stephen's Day: 26 December
For the above holidays, all shops and businesses will close (except perhaps a bakery), and they may also close on the afternoon before and the morning after. If a holiday falls on a Sunday, Monday is also a holiday. There may also be holidays for local saints' days and for regional celebrations and festivals.

Lost Property

Report lost passport to police and contact consulate. Loss of travellers' cheques should be reported to the police; contact the consulate only if stranded without money.

Money Matters

The unit of currency is the drachma – plural drachmes – abbreviated to Drs. There are coins of 1, 2, 5, 10, 20, 50 and 100 Drs, and notes of 50, 100, 500, 1,000, 5,000 and 10,000. On entry, unlimited foreign currency and travellers' cheques may be imported, though anything over ECU 10,000 (or equivalent) should be declared, enabling you to take it out again. Banks, and the post office, which now offers an exchange service for both cheques and foreign currency, have the most promising rates. For banking and post office hours, see **Opening Times**, below.

Opening Times

Greece is a law unto itself over opening times, perhaps because they are so complicated. The best one can do is state official hours and conventional norms – alongside the warning that almost everything needs checking on the day.
Archaeological Sites and Museums Hours differ from site to site, from year to year and according to the season. Summer hours, mid-March to mid-October, are longer than winter hours. Sunday hours are shorter than on a weekday. Sites and museums close entirely on some bank holidays and open for Sunday hours on others. Normally, the Irakleío and Chaniá Archaeological Museums are open daily, but the archaeological sites at Agía Triáda, Knossos, Gortyn, Gourniá, Mália and Zákros are closed Monday. Some sites remain open over the lunch hour.

It is advisable to check opening times for sites such as Knossos

Monasteries These almost always close their doors during the afternoon, usually from 14.00–17.00hrs.

Banks Monday to Friday 08.00–14.00hrs (Friday 13.30), with perhaps one duty bank re-opening its change desk from 17.30hrs in major resorts.

Post Offices Main post offices (in nome capitals): Monday to Friday 08.00–20.00hrs; special post office caravans in tourist areas also open Monday to Saturday 08.00–20.00hrs, plus Sunday 09.00–18.00hrs. Lesser post offices generally Monday to Friday 07.30–15.30hrs.

Post office exchange facilities are available at slightly different hours: normally Monday to Saturday 08.00–13.30hrs in post offices, in caravans 08.00–20.00hrs, with nothing on Sunday.

Shops Business begins early with shops opening up from about 07.00hrs. Officially, opening hours for most types of shop are Monday and Wednesday 08.00–14.00hrs, Saturday 08.00–15.00hrs. But on Tuesday, Thursday, Friday, 08.00–13.00hrs only (food shops 13.30) with afternoon opening, 17.00–20.00hrs in summer, 16.00–19.30hrs in winter. In major resorts, however, increasing numbers of shops stay open over lunch.

Personal Safety

Sunburn is the worst hazard and the most common complaint. Care must also be taken with swimming when the *meltemi* is blowing; and there are one or two underwater hazards worth mentioning – sea urchins in particular. Some kind of foot-wear may be a good idea in any event when swimming off sandy beaches. There is a poison fish which buries itself under the sand, with only its venomous spines protruding. If you should tread on one, medical help is required immediately.

Pharmacies

Found only in the larger towns and recognised by a red or green cross, pharmacists play a greater part in medical matters than they do in Britain. They are able to dispense directly some drugs and medicines only available on prescription in other countries. Codeine is banned in Greece; so are liquid painkillers. One pharmacist at least always stays open round the clock in the larger towns – details of roster posted in windows.

Places of Worship

The official religion is Greek Orthodox, with churches and chapels in great abundance. Services are often extremely beautiful and feast day services in particular are among the most important popular events on a devout island. There are Catholic churches in Irakleio, Chaniá, Réthymno and Ágios Nikólaos. There are no other Christian variants on Crete, nor is there a synagogue or active mosque.

Greek Orthodox services are held throughout Crete in churches like this one at Agía Varvára

Police

Police attitudes seem to shift with changing regimes and are currently friendly and helpful – though inevitably perhaps the police are fonder of the outwardly respectable than they are of backpackers; there is some sensitivity if an area appears to be 'going hippy'. Nobody, however, should mess around with Greek policemen,

Post Office

Each provincial capital has a major post office (recognisable by its yellow sign); major holiday towns and resorts may also have post office caravans, open for longer hours and there is a network of lesser post offices in smaller places (see **Opening Times**). Stamps are sold in post offices, of course, and also in kiosks – *periptera* – often with a small mark-up. The Poste Restante system is widely used in Greece. Send letters to the addressee, Poste Restante, at any town and they can be collected, on proof of identity (such as a passport), for a small fee. Post boxes are yellow. *Esoteriko* means inland; *exoteriko* means abroad.

Senior Citizens

Crete respects and enjoys its own older people but is not well adapted to the specialist needs of elderly visitors – nor, indeed, to the needs of the disabled. A helpful organisation is Mobility International Hellas, Egnatia 101, 8th Floor, Thessaloniki, GR54635, Greece (tel: 31 234489/206667).

particularly if indulging in sometimes tolerated but technically illegal activities like nude bathing or sleeping out. The regular police wear green uniforms, and are concerned with normal police business. The Tourist Police, a separate branch of the police force, are invariably very helpful. They are specifically trained to deal with common visitor problems and can be distinguished by their dark grey uniforms with patches in the form of national flags to indicate the languages spoken.

Student and Youth Travel

Crete is a good place for young people, as many have discovered. There are campsites, a good range of cheap rooms and youth hostels in Irakleío, Chaniá, Mália, Ágios Nikólaos, Réthymno, Siteía, Mirtios and Plakiás. Obtain Youth Hostel Association membership documents in your own country before setting out. Simple food can still be cheap on Crete and there are (limited) opportunities for work.

DIRECTORY

Telephones

For UK: 00 44 followed by British code and number less initial zero. For USA: 00 1. Codes in Crete: Irakleio, 081; Chaniá, 0821; Réthymno, 0831; Ágios Nikólaos, 0841; Siteía, 0843. Look for OTE (a separate organisation from the post office), where telephones are provided in cubicles. These are metered; you pay afterwards. Kiosks – *periptera* – often have metered telephones. In villages, the metered telephone will generally be in a *kafeneion*.

Time (Local)

Greece is two hours ahead of Britain; one hour ahead of France and other western European countries; seven hours ahead of Eastern Standard Time, US.

Tipping

Though the percentage given is sometimes quite small, Greece is a tipping country. Even the cinema usherette expects a contribution. Five to 10 per cent is appropriate in smaller restaurants (deposited on the table for table layers and lesser waiters, on the dish with the bill for the head waiter). Don't feel obliged to tip in village establishments where the owner is serving personally. Hotel dining rooms and the smarter restaurants generally include an extra 10 or 15 per cent service charge, on top of which you will probably leave any change. In hotels, tip porters and chamber-maids. In bars and cafes, leave 5 per cent or so or apply the loose change principle.

Taxi drivers, mostly owner-occupiers, do not expect tips, nor do they reject them.

Toilets

Plumbing is fine in the modern hotels, casual to a fault elsewhere. A visit to one of the rare public toilets can be a fearsome experience; cafés are often a better proposition. Steel yourself, even so, for seatless ceramic rims, perhaps in combination with dirty lavatory bowls and floors awash. In simple

After enjoying a meal out, it is customary to leave a tip

establishments, the waste paper basket by the toilet is there to collect used toilet paper.

Tourist Offices

For information before you travel, contact the National Tourist Organisation of Greece (NTOG), often known as the Greek National Tourist Organisation. There are offices in **London**: 4 Conduit Street, London W1R 0DJ; **New York**: 645 Fifth Avenue, Olympic Tower, New York, NY 10022; **Montreal**: 1233 de la Montagne, Suite 101 Montreal, Quebec, H3G 122; **Sydney**: 51–57 Pitt Street, Sydney, NSW 2000.

DIRECTORY

On Crete, the tourist organisation – here also known as EOT (Ellinikos Organismos Tourismou) – is extremely helpful. Main offices are in **Irakleío**: Xantholidou Street 1, opposite Archaeological Museum (tel: 081 228225/ 244462); **Chaniá**: 40 Kriari Street (tel: 0821 92943/92624); **Réthymno**: E Venizelou Avenue (on the beach) (tel: 0831 29148); **Ágios Nikólaos**: Akti I Koundourou 20 (tel: 0841 22357); **Siteía**: Iroon Polytechniou Square (tel: 0843 24955).

The essential beauty of Crete

LANGUAGE

Unless you know the Greek script, a vocabulary is not of very much use. But it is helpful to know the alphabet, so that you can find your way around; and the following few basic words and phrases will help too. (See also **Food and Drink**, page 99).

Alphabet

Alpha	Αα	short a, as in hat
Beta	Ββ	v sound
Gamma	Γγ	guttural g sound
Delta	Δδ	hard th, as in father
Epsilon	Εε	short e
Zita	Ζζ	z sound
Eta	Ηη	long e, as in feet
Theta	Θθ	soft th, as in think
Iota	Ιι	short i, as in hit
Kappa	Κκ	k sound
Lambda	Λλ	l sound
Mu	Μμ	m sound
Nu	Νν	n sound
Xi	Ξξ	x or ks sound
Omicron	Οο	short o, as in pot
Pi	Ππ	p sound
Rho	Ρρ	r sound
Sigma	Σσ	s sound
Taf	Ττ	t sound
Ipsilon	Υυ	another ee sound, or y as in funny
Phi	Φφ	f sound
Chi	Χχ	guttural ch, as in loch
Psi	Ψψ	ps, as in chops
Omega	Ωω	long o, as in bone

Numbers

1	éna		10	déka
2	dío		11	éndeka
3	tría		12	dódeka
4	téssera		13	dekatría
5	pénde		14	dekatéssera
6	éxi		15	dekapénde
7	eptá		16	dekaéxi
8	októ		17	dekaeptá
9	ennía		18	dekaoktó
19	dekaennía		50	peninda
20	ikosi		100	ekató
30	triánda		101	ekaton éna
40	saránda		1000	chilia

Basic vocabulary

good morning *kaliméra*
good evening *kalispéra*
goodnight *kaliníkta*
goodbye *chérete*
hello *yásou*
thank you *efcharistó*
please/you are welcome *parakaló*
yes *neh*
no *óchi*
where is ...? *poo íne?*
how much is ...? *póso káni?*
I would like *tha íthela*
do you speak English? *milate angliká?*
I don't speak Greek *then miló helliniká*

Places

street *odhós*
avenue *leofóros*
square *platía*
restaurant *estiatório*
hotel *xenodochío*
room *domátio*
post office *tachithromío*
letter *grámma*
stamps *grammatóssima*
police *astinomía*
customs *teloniakos*
passport *diavatírion*
pharmacy *farmakío*
doctor *iatrós*
dentist *odontiatrós*
entrance *isothos*
exit *éxothos*
bank *trápeza*
church *eklisia*
hospital *nosokomío*
café *kafeneion*

Travelling

car *aftokínito*
bus *leoforío*
train *tréno*

boat *karávi*
garage *garáz*
train station *tathmós*
bus station *stási ton leoforio*
airport *aerodrómio*
ticket *isitírio*

Food
food *fagitó*
bread *psomí*
water *neró*
wine *krasí*
beer *bira*
coffee *kafé*

Fish
lobster *astakós*
squid *kalamarákia*
octopus *oktapóthi*
red mullet *barboúnia*
whitebait *marithes*
sea bream *sinagritha*

Meat/poultry
lamb *arnáki*
chicken *kotópoulo*
meat balls *kefthédes*

meat on a skewer *souvlákia*
liver *sikóti*

Vegetables
spinach *spanáki*
courgette *kolokithia*
beans *fasólia*

Salads and Starters
olives *eliés*
yoghurt and cucumber dip
 tzatsíki
tomato and cucumber salad
 angoúr domáta
stuffed vine leaves *dolmádes*
'Greek' salad with cheese
 horiatiki

Desserts
honeycake *baklavá*
honey puffs *loukoumádes*
semolina cake *halvá*
ice cream *pagotó*
yoghurt *yiaourti*
shredded wheat and honey
 kataífi
custard tart *bougátsa*

With a smattering of Greek, shopping for food can be fun

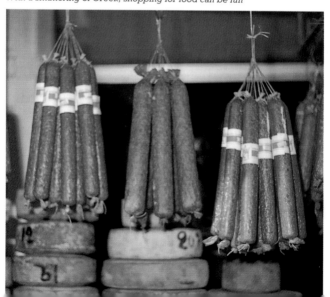

INDEX

ACKNOWLEDGEMENTS

Acknowledgements
The Automobile Association would like to thank the following photographers and libraries for their assistance in the compilation of this book:

AA PHOTO LIBRARY 13 and 41 (P Enticknap), 26 and 77 (K Patterson)

J CADY 80 Siteía.

J ALLAN CASH PHOTOGRAPHY 21 Irakleío, 70 Soúda Bay.

C GORDON 45 Réthymno inner harbour.

INTERNATIONAL PHOTOBANK 23 Market, 36 Knossos, 38/9 Mátala, 42 View from Phaistos, 49 Arkadi Monastery, 60 Handicrafts, 67 Samaria Gorge, 71 Ágios Nikólaos, 105 Cretan evening, 106/7 Taverna, 111 Donkey, 112/3 Motoring, 114/5 Dancing, 120/1 Mátala.

JOHN LLOYD 64/5 Church of Agía Roúmeli.

MARY EVANS PICTURE LIBRARY 15 Jason and the Argonauts, 18 Fighting Turks.

NATURE PHOTOGRAPHERS LTD 85 Herring gull (S C Bisserot), 86 Crocus, 87 White Mountains, 88 Cretan ebony, 90/1 Phrygana habitat (K J Carlson), 93 Green toad (P R Sterry), 94 Wood sandpiper (R Tidman), 95 Milky orchid (D T Ettlinger), 96 Spitzel's orchid (R B Burbidge), 97 Garganey (R Tidman), 98 Chameleon (M Bolton).

SPEUTRUM COLOUR LIBRARY Cover Agía Galíni, 7 Spinning, 11 Fresco, 17 Wall painting, 25 Pottery, 29 Venetian fortress, 30 café, 31 Agía Triáda, 33 Gortyn, 46 Shopping, 54/5 Chaniá harbour, 56 Chaniá, 58 Chaniá, 62 Monastery, 68 Loutró, 72/3 Washing wool, 75 Café, 78/9 Panagía Kera fresco, 82/3 Minos Beach Hotel, 88/9 Samaria Gorge, 92 Windmills, 99 Souvenirs, 100 Food, 101 Gathering grapes, 102/3 Eloúnta harbour, 110 Mopeds, 117 Knossos, 118/9 Church, 122 Sunset, 124 Irakleío.

ZEFA PICTURE LIBRARY (UK) LTD 50/1 Agía Galíni, 53 Aptera ruins.